WHO
DO YOU
THINK YOU
ARE?

❖

WHO
DO YOU
THINK YOU
ARE?

The Healing Power
of Your Sacred Self

CARLOS WARTER, M.D.

BANTAM BOOKS
New York   Toronto   London   Sydney   Auckland

Who Do You Think You Are?
A Bantam Book / March 1998

LIBRARY OF CONGRESS CATALOGING-IN-PUBLICATION DATA
Warter, Carlos, 1947–
Who do you think you are? : the healing power of your
sacred self / Carlos Warter.
p.   cm.
ISBN 0-553-10494-2
1. Spiritual healing.   2. Identity (Psychology)—Religious aspects.
I. Title.
BL624.W35   1998
299′.93—dc21   97-24738
CIP

Published simultaneously in the United States and Canada

Bantam Books are published by Bantam Books, a division of
Bantam Doubleday Dell Publishing Group, Inc. Its trademark,
consisting of the words "Bantam Books" and the portrayal of a
rooster, is Registered in U.S. Patent and Trademark Office and
in other countries. Marca Registrada. Bantam Books,
1540 Broadway, New York, New York 10036.

Printed in the United States of America
BVG   10 9 8 7 6 5 4 3 2 1

To fellow travelers on the path of spiritual inquiry at the verge of a new millennium.

To the memory of my parents and ancestors, whose lineage has allowed me to transcend the forms.

To my wife, Carolina, whose presence is the greatest gift in my daily living; and to our children, Alexandra, Charles, and David Gabriel, teachers in their own right of an expanded soul awareness.

CONTENTS

———————— ❀ ————————

PART THREE
The Face of the Divine Shines in Others
161

PART ONE

❖

Who We Are

CHAPTER ONE

—————— ❖ ——————

Widening Our Circle

Life is a sacred adventure. When we are born, it lies open to us like a 360-degree vista, waiting to be explored. As we grow up, much of what we encounter conspires to shrink this sacred circle into a tight little system that we call ourselves. As we grow older, this circle tightens and tightens until it seems that we are at the center of a very small world, a kingdom that we control and rule.

We call ourselves plumber, parent, homeowner, student, teacher, churchgoer—more than likely a combination of things—and after a while we don't venture past the limits of whatever our identity may be. We defend our territory. We let precious few people inside our circle. Yet, fortunately, throughout our lives possibilities present themselves for re-opening our circle into the bright, grand vista that was available to us as children. These opportunities often come as cataclysmic events such as illness, change, and loss, but they're also available in other ways. It is my intention in this book to show you how this transformation is available in every single moment of our lives.

At conception, we enter a material plane from some unknown realm. At birth, we establish our bodily presence in this material world. When we die, we dissolve back into that mysterious place from which we came. When we consider that unknown place—as we are forced to do when confronted with birth or death (even when it's not our own)—we may edge back in fear. Yet there is something appealing about its vastness, light, and unique openness. If we are willing to explore it, we can discover that the space exists as a liberating place in the core of our being.

That sacred space is available to us on an ongoing basis in this world, where we can feel it as vast and bright on an inner and outer level. My own experience has taught me that to reconnect with the infinite mystery and openness at the source is to meet ourselves. It is to heal by reconnecting with what is truly ours.

What does the word "sacred" conjure up for most of us? Images of cathedrals, churches, and shrines? Words spoken at baptisms, weddings, and funerals? We may recognize "the sacred" from the light cast by translucent yellow leaves framed against a gray sky in autumn. At special moments we may glimpse "the sacred" in the eyes of our beloved. Almost all of us recognize its presence at the birth of our children and at the death of our parents.

It is our birthright to open our eyes and the rest of our senses to genuinely connect with the sacred. We can do this at any time we choose, if we dare. What lies in every present moment awaiting our rediscovery is an unending universe of open, joyous, creative possibility. We are born with the means to experience it fully. This greatest and most remarkable of adventures is always available to us—if we choose to make ourselves available to *it*.

My own life has been an incredible journey of remembrance and recovery of the sacred. As a small boy I had unusual (or perhaps not so unusual, if you'll take a moment to mine your own memory) experiences that served to remind me of the open, energetic world from which we all arise. For example, after my beloved grandfather died when I was nine years old, he came to me in a dream to reassure me that he was all right in another place and that the rest of us in the family would be all right without him in this one. As I grew up, particular coincidences seemed to continually draw me beyond my everyday concerns into this world from which I came, from which we all come, and in which we even now reside. My work as a psychiatrist has allowed me to realize and engage this energy, and to understand how helpful it can be.

The world of which I speak is the world of eternal soul, a world of raw spiritual power and healing.

We think of "healing" as something to seek when we are physically or mentally ill. Some spiritual teachings would have it that we are perpetually ill—that we have committed some grave original sin from which we cannot recover. Yet I am here to tell you that on the contrary, we are perpetually, unconditionally well.

For many of us on earth, the primary task is to remember how well we really are. This book will offer you tools for healing yourself—and helping others heal themselves—to regain that place of unconditional wellness and light.

Like birth and death, essential, unconditional wellness in spite of everything is a rather frightening prospect.

Imagine considering ourselves fundamentally well even while we are dying of some dread disease. Imagine assuming—no matter what is happening to us, no matter where we are—that we are *all right*.

We have been conditioned to believe that we are *all wrong*—and that we must do something to "fix" what is inherently "broken" in us. If only we had more money, if only we ate the right foods, if only we jogged every morning, if only we had the perfect relationship, if only we had the right job, if only we were not so selfish . . . everything would be all right. And we feel guilty that it isn't.

In a variety of ways our materialistic culture, popular psychology, and (to some extent) organized religion reinforce the notion that we are "broken" from the start. We're told that we need help. So we're always trying to find a way to "fix" ourselves. We've come to accept a tacit expectation that lasting happiness is possible through the realization of our dreams of becoming rich, powerful, thin, spiritual, or *better* in any way whatsoever.

Imagine that on the conditional level, everything *is* all right. Let's say we've won the lottery. We're on the perfect diet and it shows. We raise our endorphin level every morning by jogging. We are blissfully, madly in love with our spouse, children, dog, and house. Even though we don't *have* to earn money (we won the lottery, remember?), we have meaningful work that we do because we love it and it creates benefit for everyone. Beyond that, we embody every value ever valued.

So what? In the background of the perfect life, illness and death—or maybe just death—are lurking. That's the bottom line: our lives on this material plane are going to end. We can count on it. So far, nothing in the realm of surgery or medical miracle has evolved to prevent it. If we don't want to think that far ahead, we can at least assume that our lives are going to change, whether we want them to or not. For example, we might spend that lottery money more quickly than we expected to, so we have to manage it carefully. We might pull a hamstring, and that's the end of the morning jog. What happens to our endorphin level then? Our spouse falls in love with someone else, we desire the seashore instead of the city, our children grow up, and the dog—well, his lifespan was shorter than ours anyway, wasn't it? Moreover, we feel bored with our meaningful work and we want something else to do. On top of it all, we might discover that our values aren't *our* values at all, but ones we derived from Mom and Dad, church and state, or the so-called New Age. Then we're on our own. Regardless of how these changes manifest themselves, some of them we will welcome, some we will not.

The fact is, we create worlds—and these worlds fall apart. No matter how hard we try to hold together our perfect or imperfect world, it changes. If we are attached to our world, if we identify with it, it's going to cause us grief when it disintegrates, because even if it isn't perfect, it's familiar and comforting. We try to fix our bodies and minds in a place that seems wholesome, nourishing, and happy. But everything we're talking about in this dimension—our bodies, our minds, and the environment around them—is dependent on outer conditions, like flowers are dependent on water and soil and sunlight. It's all matter. It's all material.

And what is material is subject to change. As human beings, we tend to avoid change. It's threatening. It's scary. It may be unpleasant. Even if it's pleasant, it leads us into the unknown. And the unknown is *too big* for us. We spend our conscious energy trying to cast a conceptual spell on it as if we could possibly control it. Then, in the spirit of denial to which humans are habitually accustomed, we cast it out of our circle. Because we don't entertain it, it remains a dark presence hovering in the background like an evil spirit.

Yet the unknown is where we come from when we are born, and the unknown is where we go when we die. More to the point, it's also where we go from moment to moment, if only we allow ourselves to be fully open.

I have written this book to show that going beyond our small, self-constructed circle into the unknown can be a refreshing, liberating experience. My own life has shown me that to do this may be an unpredictable process in which a key ingredient is trust. Yet to do it in a genuine way, moment by moment, is to rediscover magic within ourselves. We all have a precious opportunity to surrender to our essential self, which is not the self that we try so hard to create, sustain, and nourish. We have the opportunity to abandon the circle that we have drawn around our being, which is like a moat constructed around an ancient fortification. To face the unknown is to dissolve into the blue sky and the vast ocean beyond that fortress. This is not to say that we have to turn in our driver's license or stop cooking dinner. When we face the unknown in the ever-available moment of "now," our daily routines are enriched because we are genuinely present for them. And that genuine presence enriches anyone who comes into contact with us, no matter what we are doing.

Ironically, what we fear as the unknown is soul, which is our sacred self. To allow ourselves to move into the unknown is to heal, to become whole, to become ourselves, to become essence. To relax into the unknown is to recover the sacred; to recover the sacred is to realize ourselves as soul.

To move toward essential identity we don't have to be born again, nor do we have to die. We don't even have to get sick. I am always astonished by the fact that so many people transform their lives only after a serious illness, the death of a close friend or family member, a traumatic accident—a result of a seismic change in their lives. Why must it be this way? What happens to people who don't experience these tragedies until much later in life? Change can be a catalyst; in many respects, it should be used as a catalyst. But it is not the only catalyst. We can open our awareness to the many dimensions of our be-ing—our essential wellness—just through living our lives. In the following pages I'm going to introduce some tools and exercises for doing this. The secret of the entire pro-cess is to learn to lead with our hearts instead of our heads. There's a lot of cultural reinforcement for leading with our heads, and it ends up with people living in very small circles, crying for help in any way they see fit. On the path of heart, however, we get bigger; our circle grows. We discover a way to connect with ourselves, with soul. Then we can connect with others.

Many of us think we *have* a soul, which we might lose if we are not careful. However, on the path of heart we discover that we *are* soul. In fact, soul is a basic energy we can relax into. To do this wholeheartedly is to dis-cover the process of genuine healing.

❀ **EXERCISE** ❀
OPENING THE GIFT

Find a quiet space in your home where you will not be distracted or interrupted. Lie on the floor and relax.

Imagine that someone has given you a beautifully

wrapped gift. Visualize clearly what the wrapping paper and ribbon on the box look like. You have no idea what's inside the box. Now you are going to open it.

Remove the ribbon and tear off the wrapping paper. Open the box. Inside the box is a golden orb of light. This light moves out of the box of its own accord and rises above your head. Look at the light closely.

Now imagine that the golden globe of light contains everything you need. It contains your perfect human body, with which you can eat, drink, move, work, love, and be of service to others. This golden light also contains everything you need to live on the planet earth, including wisdom, love, and skillful means. You are self-contained in this luminous vehicle. There is nothing you need to acquire, nothing you need to buy, nothing at all that you need besides this golden light.

Let the golden light of the gift dissolve into the top of your head, and carry it with you throughout the day. When you feel inadequate in any way at all, remember your inner wealth.

CHAPTER TWO

Essence and Identity

To heal is not to cure. If it were, then true healing would not be possible, because sooner or later all of us will die. Our bodies—like automobiles, the weather, relationships—are impermanent. To heal is to become whole. To heal is to meet ourselves in an unexpected place and drop all pretensions and appearances. To heal is to choose knowledge over ignorance. To heal is to move forward and grow.

Let me give you an example. Several years ago a woman named Hilary showed up in my office. She was deeply unhappy, and as a result she had no enthusiasm for any aspect of her life. She felt sluggish and depressed, and she was concerned about her physical health. She had targeted her marriage as the root of her dissatisfaction.

Over the course of several private sessions, Hilary realized that she was suffering from her parents' negative conditioning about love. From her point of view, they had regarded each other as objects. For her mother, her father was an object of financial security. For her father,

her mother was an object of emotional security. As far as Hilary was concerned, her parents had never loved each other for what they were. They had loved each other for what they needed. Now she saw clearly that she and her husband were on the same path.

The irony of Hilary's realization became clear one September day after we had been meeting for a few months. Not only did she regard her husband as the object of her unhappiness, but she also believed that her happiness would return if she simply removed the object.

"Why do you want to get better?" I asked her.

Her face brightened, and all the hope in her heart shone through her answer. "So I can be healthy. I want to enjoy my life. I'm tired of feeling like a slug."

"Can you tell me what you see when you imagine yourself being healthy?" I asked.

She replied, "I'm having fun again. I'm not tied down. I'm free the way I was before I was married."

Instantly a darker picture came to me. Hilary had spoken freely of her previous lifestyle: late-night parties, lovers she didn't love, friends who weren't friends, recreational drugs. I had no interest in helping her return to that old way of being, and I told her as much. After all, that's how she and her husband had gotten together.

Hilary shifted uneasily and the chair creaked. "Then what do I do?"

"There is no easy answer," I replied, "no quick fix. You're seeing things with more awareness now, and no wonder that makes you feel uncomfortable. Seeing yourself clearly is not altogether pleasant, and you want to escape the discomfort by returning to something familiar. That predictable old place is like a cocoon that you spin around yourself. It may be comfortable, but it's also dark and very confining. It gets stale. This new perspective of yours is an invitation to leave your musty old comfort and explore the space beyond it. That can be scary. But there's no way that you can maintain your new awareness and run away from it at the same time."

Hilary chose not to ditch her marriage, but instead to use her new perspective as a springboard for change. The next year was one of open exploration and growth for her and her husband, who decided to support her in her efforts. Together they adopted a macrobiotic diet and started meditating. Hilary became involved in community service, making connections with people who needed her in a constructive way. Through her new activities, she attracted a caring and healthy group of friends.

If Hilary had been "cured" of her unhappiness and dissatisfaction by removing what she saw as its cause and returning to her previous lifestyle, would that have been healing?

An Awareness-Based Model of Healing

In this book I will present a new model of healing, one that does not rely on maintaining or restoring the status quo. This new model has at its root my observation that any transition—birth, sickness, death, or indeed any kind of change—can be a gateway to larger viewpoints, or dimensions of awareness. But change is not the only catalyst. Healing can occur at any time.

At the heart of the progression that I will describe is what we'll call the *essential identity*. There exists in every human being a place that is free of pain, desire, strife, disease, and fear—including the fear of death. When we discover this place, the stress and frustration that we accept as inevitable components of daily life disappear. We do not even entertain them as a possibility. This place where we are truly who we are is our essential self, or *essence*. It is the place from which we directly connect to God, love, bliss, universal energy. The essential identity is not something we have to strive to attain. It's more like a fundamental energy we are born with. As we grow up, it gets buried under habitual ways of thinking, habitual ways of acting and reacting, and self-protective tendencies. But it's always there.

The term "grownup" has a terminal ring to it. It implies that we've finished growing. We bundle our habitual patterns into an identity as good employee, parent, basketball player, "spiritual" person—and as we settle into this identity we become comfortable and stagnant. Change then becomes wrenching, something to be avoided, because we so strongly identify with who we are in the outer world.

However, if we learn to identify instead with our essential identity, we do not necessarily perceive change as a threat. Instead, we regard it as an opportunity. Outer events may swirl around us, but we can remain unthreatened and undisturbed. On the inner level this process involves tolerance, forgiveness, curiosity, and compassion for ourselves and others. On the outer level it involves taking responsibility for our state of health and making wise choices regarding the healers with whom we work.

Many of us remember our essential identity as a state of being from childhood, and all of us have accessed it at particular times. We may have glimpsed it during prayer or meditation, or in moments of heightened awareness such as orgasm, sickness, or danger. We may even have experienced it in one of those rare, radiant moments when time seems to stop, worries drop away, and we become acutely aware of the beauty and ineffability of ourselves, our companions, and our surroundings.

Whatever occasion has provided us a glimpse of the inner self, awareness of it can instill profound change. The assumption of the negativity that we thought was inevitable in ordinary existence dissolves, and the possibility for a rich and beautiful life begins to flower. When we taste this possibility, we want our lives to be that way all the time. We sense that to live fully is to live from essence.

Religions, spiritual paths, and native cultures are all rooted in this inner power. For example, recently as I was traveling through the Amazon rainforest to study with a shaman, I encountered a native tribe whose members honor the earth daily with a long, involved ritual. They regard every tree in the forest and every bird in every tree as a manifestation of the wondrous energy of earth. But their daily ceremony goes beyond making offerings to the power and bounty of the Earth Mother. It also serves to remind each participant of his or her own power and inner wealth. When I practiced Sufism intensively for some months in Morocco, I learned to recite prayers called *zhikrs* to access this inner space. My relationship with His Holiness the Dalai Lama and other Buddhist teachers has shown me that the purpose of Buddhist meditations and visualizations is to clear the route to this inner core. And in Christianity, honoring the birth of Jesus is a way of acknowledging the pure and holy space within.

Yet this place remains hidden to most of us as we go about our daily affairs. Why isn't it obvious at every moment of our lives? If it's always there, why don't we see it?

The truth is, to become even remotely aware of this power requires shifting our mental, emotional, and physical habits.

To live from essence, we must change residence. That doesn't mean going to the most remote jungle or climbing the highest mountain. On the outer level, we can live from essence anywhere. But to do so requires changing residence inwardly. It involves connecting with the energy of the divine. The human heart is the conduit for this power. The power source is God.

Everyone has a heart. Everyone wants love. Our true vocation is love. The core frequency that unites us all is love, and it flows through the heart. Wellness—spiritual, emotional, and physical—is related to our ability to open our hearts to God, which happens when we live from essence.

Overall health is a function of the balance between head and heart. The head transmits information. The heart activates wisdom. In this age of information, it is easy to forget about the function of the heart. The brain reaches our awareness with feelings, sensations, and imagery. The heart's communication is much more subtle. We hear the heart through the inner voice of silence—that quiet, still place from which creativity, inspiration, and deep kinds of knowing originate. The brain sorts, categorizes, analyzes. These are important activities, but when they take precedence over the perceptions of the heart, we become disoriented.

It's odd that we can forget the heart's intelligence when so many of our common expressions point to it: "I know it by heart." "In my heart of hearts, I believe it." "She spoke to me straight from the heart." "I can't believe how cold-hearted we've become." "Let's get to the heart of the matter." Living from essence is a heart-centered approach. Like the space between heartbeats, essence is an infinite inner territory untouched by outer events. Like our hearts, it is rhythmic and pulsating and warm. It is as free-flowing as a mountain stream. It is not born, it doesn't die, and it cannot be controlled. It has a natural intelligence, an innate wisdom, a perpetual energy. It permeates everything. What we think, feel, eat, drink, or buy has nothing to do with essence. Yet it is present in every moment.

No matter what name we give this divine energy, we glimpse it in moments of essential awareness, and we start searching for it. The name we give the greater power to which we pray does not affect the end result of the process of dissolving crystallized temporary identities. The end result of dissolving temporary identities is that we are who we are, our sacred self.

Do you believe in Christ, the Buddha, Yehora Allah, the Goddess, no one, love, or just a universal power? When you say "Oh Lord," you are simply recognizing that we're in the context of something that is bigger than us. What is bigger than us is the aspiration that calls to us, draws us to it magnetically, outside our bubble of survival. Sometimes the search is external. Sometimes it turns inward. That drive can be seen as spiritual or conscious evolution. It is similar to but not tied to the force of biological evolution.

For some reason we can envision evolution occurring in the timespan of generations, but when we consider personal or conscious evolution, we seem to think it stops when we reach adulthood. What leads us to think we stop evolving? The force that mysteriously leads the sperm toward the ovum and on through stages of embryo, fetus, baby, child, teen, adult, and sage—an eternally traveling consciousness—how could it stop? The

poet and teacher of Sufism Mevlana Jallaludin Rumi
wrote of the consciousness we now experience as starting with "stone consciousness," that is, the state of
awareness of rocks. He said that we progress from there
to plant, animal, and human consciousness, and then to
angel, archangel, and beyond.

My approach to healing involves surrendering to the
force of conscious evolution. To do that, we need to give
up the illusion that we are in control.

In Christianity, Jesus tells us that no one goes to the
Father without going through His son. In Islam, we are told
to extinguish ourselves in Allah. In Hinduism, we are ex-
horted to "surrender the reins of our life." All these traditions recognize the paradox of things improving when
we stop trying to make them better. Fortunately, when we
focus on our heart, surrender is no longer something we
have to achieve through struggle. It comes naturally.

Our planet has suffered from a long sleep disorder.
Now we have the opportunity to truly wake up. It is not a
"sin" that we have slept, but a long-held illusion. We
were babies; we were innocent. We believed the first
thing presented to us was an identity. And we continue to
take on false identities. We learn to identify with something that is not our true self. It takes us years and years
to find out that the identity we believed in is not us.

Imagine if your beloved mother and father had recognized their own essential identity and thus were able to
tell you, "Kathleen, we're calling you by a name because
in third-dimensional reality we need to be able to call
each other by name. But you are not simply your name.
Who you are is much more than your name, or your
neighborhood, or your country, or the color of your skin,
or your occupation.

"Who you are is a majestic, perfect, delightful, spiritual being whose purpose in entering this world is to learn the transformation of matter into the brilliant light that is service. Through knowing this, you will leave this place vibrating at a higher resonance, at a lighter wavelength, than when you entered it. Know that even though you are unique, everyone has the same purpose, and the same essential identity to realize."

Can you imagine growing up in that context of sacredness? Can you imagine not having to spend years trying to recover the sacred and rediscover yourself simply because there was a slight error of description when you first met your parents, teachers, and friends in the third dimension? Imagine how you would feel in terms of self-esteem and self-knowledge, had you grown up with that kind of information instead of, "Kathleen, you're American, you're white. Anything that's not white and not American is not part of us. You belong to our family and our neighborhood, and anything else is bad."

When identity is defined by outside parameters, our early childhood development is distorted. Our divinely given brain begins to contract. Our circle tightens. It speaks to itself and says, "This area of the brain we don't need. We don't need intuition, extrasensory perception, or cosmic consciousness. We just need to be robots. We just need to produce and survive. Nothing but survival matters." That's how fear of nonsurvival begins.

Here we are, grownups who did not receive the truthful information about essence—human beings who were not given the substantial activation to be themselves, to move toward the light. Here we are, looking to prove to each other that prayer is valuable, that meditation is beneficial, that yoga is good.

We must wake up, because we are in a state of emergency. I sincerely know that we are in an emergency moment in planetary evolution. We've heard it before: we are in a crisis moment. We need to get rid of the shackles of sociological and biological conditioning. We don't need to prove to anyone that prayer works. It is by the manifestation of prayer that humanity has been brought into action. It was the word of God made flesh; it was the prayer of God, that vibration, that manifested us.

It is time to open our hearts and say *"Muchas gracias,* thank you very much." Gratitude opens a doorway of interdimensional voyaging. When gratitude sets in, we relax, we smile. We can be content. We have enough. Our hearts open.

We need to seriously regard our life as precious. We need to begin to tune in to the majesty that we embody so that we remember our true identity—the identity of essence.

What is the identity of essence? It's very simple. Is one chair the same as another? Yes and no. If we say that each has four legs and is made of wood, then we can say they're the same. If we say, "This one has cloth, the other one doesn't," then they're different. Are they identical? Will they ever be identical? No.

This chair is identical with itself, only and forever, correct? So are you.

It's hard to hear this, because in the sleep state we say, "Of course, I know that. So what? Big deal." But if we were truly to understand that we are identical only to ourselves, a unique phenomenon in the history of the cosmos, we would understand this simple transmission. We would start vibrating and spinning inwardly with such a joy that we would start leaping around the room!

But we can't understand that we are a cosmic phenomenon unique to ourselves because we live "in our heads." Our mindset identifies with our history, our culture, our race, our religion, our biography. Have our history, culture, race, religion, and personal biography been ecstatic at all times? No. In fact, the history of humanity has been plagued by wars, destruction, disease, death, decay, and survival.

We are at a crossroads today. We either shift the paradigm of our identity from our heads to our hearts and become happy to be alive beyond whatever happened in the history of the human race, or we use once again this perpetual life force to reassert our collective story line and remain in the static state of the status quo.

We can stop identifying with our temporary being—with our path of the head—and recognize our essential identity. We can recognize that we're unique.

Of course, we have to give up a lot to become unique. We have to give up who we *think* we are. But that's not a problem. It's very easy. Through realizing what we are, we know what we are not. We are not our bodies, we are not our emotions, we are not our intellects. We are essence.

We must give up a false sense of personal control. In that moment of surrender, something happens. A remembrance of something familiar happens, something that took place frequently when we were children. There is joy, a sense of "Ah-hah!" This joy has a body that looks just like the body we inhabit here in the third dimension, but the joy body is transparent—it is light, not heavy. It is hollow, not solid. It is a delight. This is fourth-dimensional energy: still dualistic and separate, but more expanded.

An Interdimensional Process

Between consensus reality (identification with the darkness of matter) and unity consciousness (identification with the light of essence), there are a number of levels. These are degrees of awareness, not spiritual goals. They are how we open our feelings, hearts, and senses to the way of the living universe.

All these dimensions exist right now, as you hold this book in your hands. If we are aware of them, we can move freely among them. Opening to the highest levels of awareness allows us the freedom of seeing all the other dimensions with panoramic vision. When we operate from the transcendent, luminous, nondualistic realm of the fifth dimension, we know the invisible four-dimensional energy of the living world, and at the same time we can operate beautifully in the material plane of the third dimension (eating, sleeping, taking care of business, etc.). But the environment in which we operate is radically different when our awareness is *limited* to that of the third dimension. With expanded awareness, our hearts are completely open while we are operating in the third dimension. Because we know that we are essence, we no longer have need of third-dimensional defenses. In essence, there is nothing to defend. The world and the soul come together. The present moment holds all.

I use these dimensions as a model simply to stimulate understanding of our inner processes as we move toward essence. We must remember that models by their very nature do not accurately reflect reality.

THE THIRD DIMENSION

The third dimension is bound by time and space. It is the material dimension, the most ordinary and visible of realities. This is the dimension in which we as souls have bodies, the dimension in which we experience our lives on earth.

The third dimension is the dimension of "objective reality." It is possible to prove scientifically that this dimension "exists." At least it is possible to describe it in scientific language, to analyze it and document it, to measure its most subtle elements in time and space. But there are higher dimensions of existence, and we're in them *right now*. We just don't necessarily see them with our eyes. Like horses, we've put on blindfolds so that we see only with our physical eyes.

One reason that we can measure life in the third dimension is that it is *dualistic*. In this dimension we see ourselves as separate from everything else, and indeed we appear to be so.

In third-dimensional reality it is easy to identify with the small story. There is nothing unseen, no proof of interconnection or inner power or an inner life. In this objective, dualistic reality our tendency is to see everything as an object.

Because we're trying to attract pleasure and avoid pain, we try to control and manipulate the "objects" around us: our own experience, other people, even the resources of the earth. We feel sympathy but not empathy. When we feel spaciousness, warmth, spontaneity, or generosity, we might label it as some kind of peak experience, put it in our pockets, and take it out on holy days to admire it.

Love that we feel in this dimension is conditional; it is

based on material exchange: "Mom and Dad will love me if I do what they want me to do." "God will love me if I'm good." "I will love you if you will be who I want you to be."

Since we are ignorant of an inner life in this dimension, we naturally look outward for signs that we are worthy of love. Like Snow White's wicked stepmother, we find ourselves asking those around us, "Mirror, mirror, on the wall—who's the fairest of them all?" Often, what results is called a relationship:

"Hi, Lou, I'm worth nothing, I'm miserable, I'm no one. Now tell me something good about me so I can love you."

"You're cute."

"Oh, thank you very much, now I'm totally dependent."

The nature of our work in this realm is that we do whatever is in front of us. Thus, it is possible to exist in the third dimension without ever looking up. If we do look up, we may find the space around us so shocking in its vastness that we quickly look back down.

When we identify with third-dimensional reality our experiences, concepts, and beliefs define the parameters of reality. It's difficult to trust our inner experience, because we can't prove it. So we look for outer confirmation that it happened.

Because we have not yet discovered our inner authority, we remain attached to outside authority. It might be the internalized voices of Mom and Dad, or the voice of our boss or our spouse, or even God. We might be rebelling against it; we might be submissive to it. Either way, our engagement with outer authority keeps us from taking full responsibility for who we are.

In third-dimensional awareness, we sometimes have

the feeling that nothing will ever change. We're sedated by heavy illusion, supported by a solid material realm. Luckily it's shot through and through with wonderful opportunities to wake up to who we really are. These include impermanence, the stress of defending our ego-bubble, and the suffering we feel from resisting the natural flow of life when we don't want things to change.

The mental body becomes very strong in the third dimension. We are interested in information rather than essence. Information is safe. Feeding our heads with information is one way to avoid contact with our bodies, our feelings, and the world around us.

With a strong mental story line, we weave ourselves into a world of concepts and judgments. Our internal narrative keeps what might disturb us at a distance. It is easier to "think" the world than to open our hearts to the world of sensations.

For example, we can understand the scientific process of photosynthesis. But try wrapping your brain around the outright mystery of a tree—and the miracle of humans' complementary relationship with the tree! We can easily measure the speed of light. But the vastness of the universe—and how small we are within it—is almost impossible to comprehend intellectually. We can tell someone how to make bread, but can we put the smell of it baking into words?

It's possible to so confine ourselves to mental concepts in this dimension that we're unlikely to feel much curiosity. Our best friend may relate a problem of dramatic proportions, but rather than ask questions we simply say, "I know what you mean. That reminds me of the time when I . . ."

Our favorite response in this dimension is, "I know."

I don't mean to imply that limiting our awareness to

the world of the third dimension is necessarily pleasurable. In fact, it can be intensely claustrophobic. When our vision is this small, our hearts are closed not only to the infinite space beyond but also to the infinite space within. Yet there is comfort even in pain, as long as the pain is familiar and we have a favorite, familiar way to forget it.

In a culture of socially acceptable anesthetics, it's easy to find a way to forget. When the third-dimensional view is solid, fear for survival can be so strong that we habitually retreat into whatever makes us feel comfortable, safe, and good. We're afraid to face the world outside our circle. This process is inherently stressful because it requires constant defense.

It's not that retreating into whatever reduces our world to a manageable size is bad. For example, there was a time when I simply didn't leave my house unless my heart was open. But there's a difference between retreat from a big-story perspective and a small-story perspective. In one we retreat out of awareness of our needs, and in the other we retreat out of a habitual fear response. One comes from aware direction, and the other comes from habitual reaction. That says a lot about the difference between the small vision of the third dimension and the bigger vision of the fourth and fifth.

When we are beginning to stir from the sleep-state of the third dimension, several pitfalls can obstruct our expanding awareness.

First, we might take a materialistic approach to whatever jolts us awake from our limited third-dimensional viewpoint. Or we might become fascinated with our ability to control and manipulate our thoughts. We might try to use our newfound power to dominate others. This could become an obstacle to any kind of transition. We might also solidify affirmations or positive thinking by using them in a material way—trying to heal ourselves from physical illness or attract a lot of money, for example.

Or we might become disillusioned. Our expectations of physical or spiritual perfection are not met by our shift in awareness. We're surprised that in our expanding awareness we still experience pain. We expected to be "fixed" or "saved." It turns out that we were looking for just one more way to live "happily ever after."

Fortunately, confronting our ideals in the third dimension without a big-story purpose will lead to disappointment—which is another gateway to essential identity, another opportunity to wake up.

THE FOURTH DIMENSION

The fourth dimension coexists with the purely physical, mechanical world bound by time and space. It opens with our knowing that we are more than material manifestation points. Whenever and however that opening occurs, the world becomes a bigger place. This is the dimension of the spiritual seeker.

As the sleepiness of the third dimension begins to clear, we see that no longer must we do what we think will make Mom and Dad happy. We've heard the whisper of an inner voice, and we begin to listen to it. With heightened self-awareness we begin to take responsibility for our lives.

As our awareness expands we see that we've been profoundly conditioned by what we believe. We see that we've been programmed to accept without question the constructed truths and realities of science and society. We see that we've been confined by our "mental body," which consists of the stories about reality that we tell ourselves and others.

Our confining bubble of ego is stretched, and now we see the potential to go beyond it. The possibility of inner work arises in us, perhaps for the first time. With this viewpoint, we may seek out a guru or spiritual teacher. We long for someone to show us our inner self, to show us how to make our hearts sing.

As our perception changes, so does our world.

We begin to feel space. As we feel space, we begin to feel more spacious, more generous, more spontaneous, more curious. "Who knows?" replaces the "I know" of third-dimensional awareness.

We might now become aware of psychic phenomena and past lives. We start to pay attention to dreams, intuition, coincidences, synchronistic events, and other "unscientific" ways of knowing. We trust our inner experience. As we become aware of the invisible dimensions, we might also begin to feel the waves of love and energy that activate the living world.

For guidance, we are now more apt to turn to our inner voice than to outside authority. We might realize that most of what we thought we wanted is not what we wanted at all. We clear the decks, clean the house, get rid of physical, mental, and psychological clutter. We live "in the world," but we are no longer "of the world," as St. Paul wrote.

We make the move from "doing" to "being." We see that we don't have to do it all; it is all done. From that a maturity arises to learn to manage ourselves from the perspective of essence—who we really are. A larger, mystical sense of self dawns in our awareness.

Our perspective is still dualistic in that we imagine ourselves as separate from other forces of the universe. Although our ego-bubble might have stretched or even popped, we now have a "watcher," or an "inner witness," who tells us how we're doing. The world is still divided into good and evil, us and them.

Our experience of love is still conditional. At this point, however, it might be based on magnetic attraction. We are drawn to those with whom our hearts resonate. The resonance we experience will allow our hearts to open further.

We become clear about why we are here; we become actively engaged with our higher purpose. Although we are still working on personal issues, our lives are now less about "cleaning up our act" and more about fulfilling our purpose and making the contribution we were put on earth to make. We want to wake up fast and to help others wake up fast, too. As we no longer grasp at our temporary identities, we begin to know that we are multi-dimensional beings. We can open further and let the energy of the universe flow through us. Along the same lines, we become aware of negative thought patterns—which are like muscle spasms of mental activity—and learn to release them as well.

If our hearts are open enough to also feel compassion, self-love, and forgiveness, we might also be able to *accept our condition*. We can recognize guilt, blame, or shame and let it go. In the silence of the heart that follows, gentleness arises. We accept ourselves as we are and extend ourselves lovingkindness.

THE FIFTH DIMENSION

In the fifth dimension we function as "I am," the container for our body, mind, spirit, and joy. We regard being on this planet as being in a state of grace. The spiritual path opens wide. Worlds of alignment take place as we stabilize our third-dimensional, material being in the knowledge of essence. Our body, speech, mind, and purpose are synchronized.

Our circle of ego is gone, and so is our watcher. We no longer identify with our material manifestation or see ourselves as separate. There are no obstacles to continuing discovery of other levels of awareness. This is the growth of the tree called human.

Now we are fully embodied. We function in unified fields of energy. Inner knowing, not outer authority, is our standard of measurement for what is real. This is a quantum leap. We have a feeling of certainty, knowing, power, and completeness. No longer trying to attract or avoid anything along the way, we let our lives unfold like a divine drama.

We are multidimensional beings who identify with nothing and with everything. We do not even identify with essence; we *are* essence. We are thoroughly blended into the universal energy of essential relationship—interconnectedness.

Because we have passed beyond self-limiting beliefs, our hearts are completely open, receptive of the energy of divine love that bathes the universe. We are like a mirror reflecting the sun. In Buddhism this state is known as the "bliss body." In Christian mysticism it is known as "Christ consciousness." In Kabbalah it is known as *yehida,* which means "unity" or "uniqueness."

Now our vision is broad. There is no duality, no illusion of good and evil, no us and them. We are intent, directed, and clear in our being. We know who we are; we can remember who we are. We also have the ability to master what happens in our consciousness moment by moment. Mastery has replaced control. We can direct the energy of our thoughts, actions, or words either toward heaven or toward earth.

For example, the early fathers of the Christian church dissolved their spiritual energy into air as they went into the desert to live lives of contemplation. St. Francis of Assisi concentrated the same kind of energy into an earth-bound material manifestation—the forming of the Franciscan orders.

In this dimension, empathy, humor, and unconditional joy predominate. Faith in the continuity of our essential being has replaced fear of death and loss of soul. We know the infinite love surrounding us and the infinite space within. We have relaxed into who we are.

We wake up each morning grateful for being awake and alive. Everything we experience—our thoughts, feelings, irritations, activities, mishaps, and encounters—is the embodiment and flow of divine energy.

How I Discovered Essence

I remember when I was one year old, sitting in a tall yellow wooden chair at my birthday party. I know my awareness is real: I was surrounded by my family, my aunts and uncles, who were all saying the usual things that grownups project onto babies. "My, how he's grown!" "Isn't he the spitting image of so-and-so?"

At the end of the table on the right was my grandfather, who was in his early eighties. To me, this man was a very beautiful being. I looked into his clear blue eyes, and I felt a wave coming back from him that woke me up forever.

I knew I was not my body. I knew this celebration was

not about my tall chair. It was definitely not about how I
had grown. I knew that I *was*. I knew that I *am*. I knew
that *he* was. That we were what? That we were life! That
we were life organizing and expressing itself according to
pictures of our particular reality.

I have kept that knowledge to this day. Through that
awareness, I woke up. From then on, I tried to put that
knowledge to practical use. When my parents got mad at
me, for example, I wouldn't believe them. I learned and
grew from my mistakes, but I knew they weren't mad at
me. You don't get mad at a soul.

Let's go back again to when we were little children.
Imagine that your mother says to you, "Henry, who you
are is light. Who you are is concentrated love force. Who
you are is the purest, sweetest honey of the essence of
God herself. Who you are has come through me, and
though I am your mother, I really am your peer. Because
who I am is a joyful essence who has now been able to
see the miracle of life coming through me. And I am here
to serve you and remind you that your destiny and my
destiny are the same. It is the destiny of infinite ecstasy."

To be practical (as we say in third dimensional language), we have to learn to walk, talk, move, see, define,
and name certain things. We have to experience boundaries and learn how to function within them. But remember, the only purpose of our being here in this material
existence is the spiritualization of matter, the conscious
movement of matter toward the light. This is also called
creativity. It involves taking spiritual energy and moving
it into matter.

The Kabbalah speaks of worlds within worlds. First
there is being, then there is doing. That is how we bring
spiritual energy into formation. Medical technology, for
example, is ultimately the manifestation of the spirit in

matter via intellectual understanding. It involves taking our basic desire as humans to help those among us and *materializing* it into pharmaceuticals, diagnostic technologies, and surgical techniques.

The materialization of spirit happened already by divine will: we were born. When the heart opens, we experience higher emotions; from these come virtues and values. Now we can spiritualize the matter, play with it, and serve each other—because everyone is differently, uniquely engaged in the same purpose, or job. Our job is that of perfecting creation through the balance of human and divine intelligence.

I work with people. I serve as a medical doctor because through medicine I feel that I can help activate people to move from the darkness of pain, crisis, and chaos to the light of healing and inner peace. I feel compassion for the pain and suffering of others and have a profound desire to alleviate it. This is my fundamental calling.

I also express myself as an educator because I know that the power of reason can help people shift from false identifications to essential identity. However, I have discovered that sometimes where pain doesn't work as a teaching, reason also doesn't work. It's like watching someone who is hammering a nail and keeps hitting his finger. You say, "Move the hammer an inch to the right!" But the person keeps hammering the same old way because he can't hear you.

I am also a messenger of love. This is another way in which I choose to be present. In this particular function, I don't have to push so very hard. I can simply be my message. Every once in a while I find that someone gets the message and experiences something that resonates with what I'm saying. "If I'm unique, I'd better dedicate my life to fully finding out the bliss territory in which I exist—because I've never happened in exactly this way before, and no one else has happened like me, and never will I happen again. Even in a biological sense, this organization of DNA is never going to repeat itself. Even twins are different."

I move fluidly between these identities—and many others—and find that because I know what I really am, I can perform these functions with passion, love, and efficiency without being stuck in any of them.

In Search of Essence

Many people who have had a glimpse of essential identity attend my workshops and talks. They come for insights into the process of living from that inner place, as well as for tools for maintaining contact with essence. Learning to live from essence is the process I have been helping people with in one form or another throughout my entire life. Those who have had an experience of it become transformed into positive-seeking human beings.

It always impresses me how many different ways my students have of describing the quest that they are on:

> "Since I have glimpsed the depth of who I am, something in my daily life experience seems to be missing."

> "Now that I know what openness is available to me at a fundamental level, I will do anything it takes to learn to live in it."

> "All my life, I have missed what I've always known deep inside is possible."

"After my aunt died, I grieved a lot and my heart seemed to open up. I had the strangest feeling of being one with the universe. But then came another kind of shock—my husband left me—and I closed off again. How can I regain the feeling that we are all connected?"

"I would like to make a difference in the world, but I'm only one person."

"Even though I've been involved with health and healing for years, I feel that my involvement is mechanical. I feel as if I'm dealing with the surface of things instead of making true contact. As an instrument of healing, my whole heart seems to need to express itself in a more genuine way."

Hope, Fear, and "Happily-Ever-After"

The purpose of human life, I believe, is to be happy. If we take a moment to examine our concepts of happiness, we'll find that this statement is more simple than it sounds.

What makes us happy? Most of us are happy when we get what we want, when others praise us, when we feel cherished and loved. In other words, we are happy when pleasure comes our way.

It's safe to say that human beings everywhere strive to attract pleasure. At the same time, we try to avoid pain and loss of all kinds. It is hard to imagine anyone feeling the other way around.

The conventional notion of happiness involves a delicate dance of attraction and avoidance. In this dance, we try to attract what makes us happy while at the same time trying to push away what might cause us unhappiness. As long as we continue this jittery dance, selecting which people, events—even feelings—we like and which ones we don't, we will continue to live in the small world that most of us inhabit.

This "happily-ever-after" feeling that most of us seek is not the kind of happiness connected with realizing our essential identity. In fact, "happily-ever-after" is intimately connected with the hope that we will keep what makes us happy, and the fear that we will lose it. Such an idea of happiness is bound up not only with what we have but also with who we *think* we are.

This materialistic approach extends toward health and healing. On a deep level we believe that lasting good health is our right. We believe that every disease, every disorder, has a "cure" if only we can find it. Health and healing are seen as a matter of protecting the status quo, not exploring the new horizons that any change can open.

At the heart of the materialistic approach is a blind belief in and dependence on externals. Hand in hand with that belief is an ignorance of one of the most documentable and basic truths of existence on this planet, the truth of *impermanence*. Everything changes, all the time.

This fact can be seen at every level of activity, where it is as profound as it is simple. Take an ice cube out of the freezer and watch it change into water. Drive your car and experience what happens as gas changes into energy. Even the cells of our bodies are changing: although you may feel that you are exactly the same person you were seven years ago, within this period of time all the cells in your body have died and regenerated themselves.

Impermanence is so basic to our existence that most of us just chug right along in blind ignorance of it, striving for the lasting happiness promised in fairy tales. As we depend on externals and refuse to acknowledge imper-manence, we neglect to cultivate the richest, most pre-cious possibility that is open to us as human beings: connecting to the happiness that arises when we realize our essential identity.

A Bigger Kind of Happiness

When I say that I believe the purpose of life is to be happy, it is that inner happiness of which I speak. It is the happiness that comes from *waking up* to who we are. It is the happiness that comes from discovering that we were never "broken" in the first place.

As a psychiatrist, I have witnessed many people under-going what I call an "Ah-hah!" experience, a break-through in which they rediscover their essential well-being. I realized long ago that people do not come to a workshop or to therapy to learn a new conceptual model of health. They come to wake up to themselves.

Remembering our essence involves seeing that we have focused on the wrong targets, which drains our en-ergy and causes us to feel inadequate. For example, many times in relationship counseling I have come up against a client's idea that without her "other," she is somehow broken. It's easy to forget that we are each always whole.

The happiness that comes from inner wholeness is not at all connected with external conditions. Nor is it subject to the ravages of time. It is self-existing within us. To most of us it is also self-secret. We have to work hard to discover it. Its source is essence. It is not simply some-thing we *possess* but our own true nature, untouchable by the passage of time—the nature of being awake to the holiness of our human selves and our unique connection to divine energy.

Essence is an outer territory, too. It's the energy of the universe. The essential self—where our healing power comes from—is like the seed of that energy. To become aware of that seed and let it open is to invite ourselves to connect with this greater energy.

In Taoism the essential force or field is known as Tao, and the *Tao Te Ching* speaks of it as being "smaller than an electron" yet containing "uncountable galaxies." In Buddhism it is known as dharma, a sort of law under which everything in the universe is governed. Many religions and sacred traditions see this all-pervasive force as God or Allah or the Great Spirit or the universal mind.

Life Living Life

We might think that since essence is eternal, it is cold, hard, and unmoving, like a glacier or the Rock of Gibraltar. Interestingly enough, however, it is just the opposite.

The natural energy of essence is evolutionary. Whether we choose to practice connecting with essence or continue to completely ignore it, it propels us forward. It propels us to grow and it propels us to open. It is the energy of life living life. What arises from this energy is different from the ordinary kind of happiness that we *hope* to keep and *fear* to lose. This kind of happiness is a free-flowing joy that is open and accepting of our movement through time and space. It thrives on true contact and direct connection with all the other forces—both seen and unseen—in the universe.

Living in a state of true openness and connection without hope and fear may sound like an impossible dream. However, it is quite possible, as a human being, to live from the place called essence. Throughout history, spiritual leaders such as Jesus Christ, Muhammed, the Baal-Shem-Tov, and the Buddha have demonstrated that it is possible. There are people in this century who have lived from this place: the Dalai Lama and Mother Teresa come quickly to mind. Many lesser-known people have lived and are living from this place, whether we call it enlightenment, bliss, heaven, or sainthood. It is the state of awakeness that results from seeing through our belief in temporary identities and surrendering to who we truly are. Surrendering in this way opens us to receiving the divine love of the universe. It also lets us radiate that energy to others.

Living from essence is not an experience available only to people we consider "spiritual." It is a path available to each of us every day, every hour, every moment. To access it requires some practice and determination. It is like a wavelength on a radio dial. We have the choice to keep our tuner there or not. And sometimes even if we are "tuned in" to essence, we experience a lot of static.

In brief, our essential identity is the certainty and the oneness of being that is at the center of all experiences. It is the common denominator or reference point that is experienced as "I Am." It's not "I am this profession," "I am this race," "I am this type of believer," or any smaller, more specific identifications. I am. I exist. It is what we are from childhood through old age, and it can even transcend the limits of time.

Essence is true wealth and true medicine. The trouble is, most of us live as if we don't know it's there.

❀ EXERCISE ❀
LIVING IN THE MOMENT OF NOW

Clear a space in your home where you can be alone with a clock. The size of the clock doesn't matter—it could be a wristwatch—but make sure that it has a second hand.

Find a comfortable chair from which you can see the clock. Now, as you watch the second hand make its rounds, repeat the word "now." Repeat the word "now" until you feel completely one with the second hand on the clock. Repeat the word "now" until you feel that you are residing in your own heart. Repeat the word "now" until your body feels at some distance from you and you feel a flame beginning to burn in your heart. Now feel yourself resting on the chair, feel the space that exists between the word "now" and the chair and the clock and the room. Feel the light that comes out from your body. When you stop repeating the word "now," how does the room look?

CHAPTER THREE

❖

The Big Story Versus the Small Story

The truly impossible dream is the conventional happiness that most of us seek. We imagine being in a state of physical and material perfection, safe from illness, death, or any other kind of pain. We desire a solid, unmoving place—just the opposite of what we are, which is essence. So we try to create that kind of place for ourselves—a reference point—by telling ourselves little stories about whatever is happening to us. No matter how big it is, we try to make it small enough to fit into our ego-bubble. And we try to hold our bubble firm, forgetting that it is fundamentally impossible to find a solid, unmoving place, either physically or psychologically. As we spend our lives trying to establish such a place, our hearts lose the elasticity that comes from being open to the divine love that is ours to receive and to recycle.

The conflict between our desire for "fixed" security and happiness, coupled with the basic truth of impermanence and evolution, produces friction and stress. In turn, friction and stress produce all kinds of ill health—emotional, spiritual, or physical.

Ego-Bubbles and the Barnacles of Illusion

How have we forgotten essence? Why do we habitually resist what we are?

When a baby is conceived, the light and wisdom of universal energy develop into a human being. Over a span of nine months two cells multiply into a trillion, and the result is the marvelous, intricate mechanism that is the human body. Physically, spiritually, intellectually, at birth we are who we are and we *know* who we are.

Our nature at birth is the nature of essence—open, receptive, and radiant—pure divine love. Our basic impulse as newborns is to love and be loved.

As we look around for reflections of this unconditional love, most of us, however, find something else. The world into which we are born has almost universally forgotten the essential connection. It's as if we as humans have forgotten the meaning of humanity.

If essential connection is the universal currency, being born is like coming into the world with lots of money but no place to spend it. We find ourselves looking into the eyes of mothers and fathers or other caregivers who have long ago forgotten who they truly are. They have lost touch with their own connection to essence. Without the ability to see themselves in this deeper light, it is impossible for them to see us in this light.

As a result of looking into the faces of those who have forgotten their essence, we begin to believe that who we are is not acceptable. We notice that we are loved only if we behave in a particular way—for example, when we are quiet, when we do what our parents tell us, when we are amusing, or when we don't exercise our natural predilection for exploration and curiosity. Based on the feedback we are given, we decide that we are not valued as ourselves, not worthy of unconditional love.

Because giving and receiving love is our primary motivation, we soon set out to discover ways by which we can become "worthy" of love. As children, even very young children, we learn to assess each situation and then make decisions about who we need to be in order to find acceptance and love and a sense of belonging. Our basic motivation is to be who we need to be in order to get the love we need. Being who we think the world wants us to be becomes a habitual pattern.

This is the currency of conditional love: "You be who I want, and I will love you."

These beliefs, assumptions, and decisions about who we *need* to be begin to form around who we truly *are* like barnacles on a ship's hull. Our essence becomes obscured, and we forget who we are. We develop "personality." As we grow and develop further, we make more and more decisions and form more and more beliefs based on what happens as we live our lives.

You fall in love; you get hurt. You'll never fall in love so hard again. You trust a friend; your friend betrays you. You don't trust people so easily after that. Or maybe your friend does not betray you, and you trust everyone. You become gullible, and people take advantage of you. Then you regard yourself as a fool.

Whatever happens to us, the layers around our essential being become thicker and more impermeable. Our hearts begin to close. We forget our conscious connection with the natural flow of divine love in and through our lives. We forget the inner peace, wisdom, and wholeness of essence at our core. We learn to look outside for these things as we become more and more identified with the crusty layers around essence—the personality we developed based on who we thought we needed to be in order to be loved. All too soon, we regard these layers of crust—our self-image—as "us." All of us.

THE CRUST THICKENS

Our bodies come from "nowhere" before birth and after death dissolve into the elements. It is quite strange that even in the face of this great mystery most of us develop the attitude that our body is "ours" or "us," and that we are our body.

We also begin to identify with our thoughts, regarding them as "us" and "ours." It is possible to identify with them so strongly that we spend much of our lives being ignorant of our surroundings while indulging in our inner "story line." Living in our heads allows us to have any number of fantastic experiences while we shut out the only experience that is truly ours: the experience of the present moment.

The same thing happens with our emotions, which are thoughts amplified. We solidify them into something monumental and important, into "I love" and "I hate," and we take the energy of the emotion to be ourselves. We are willing to invest in it heavily. How many wars have been fought on the solid ground of "I love" and "I hate"?

Having engineered our own self-image, we regard even our soul as solid—something we "have" that we could therefore lose. In fact, soul—essence—is what we are, and we cannot lose what we are. But because we forget the infinite energy that we embody and instead identify with what is finite, we live in fear of loss. This is not a sin, but an illusion that comes simply from having forgotten who we are.

THE PATH OF THE HEAD

Our self-image is fabricated from limitations and restrictions. And because every aspect of our small world is finite, it is all subject to change. Nevertheless we draw these boundaries tightly around ourselves in a fortress that we learn to call "me." Having invested so much energy resisting the natural urge of the heart to stay open, having invested so much energy in drawing our boundaries, we now attempt to control our world. We let in only what will reinforce our fortress. We try to keep out anything that would cause us to question what we have so carefully built. It is not the path of the heart that comes into play here, but the path of the head.

In an effort to control our world we conceptualize, judge, label, and thus essentially deny it. It takes a great deal of mental energy to shrink our world to a manageable, defendable size. We even do this in the name of knowledge by acquiring a few tools and a few bits of data, and then we fall asleep and automatically repeat the same thing because it works. If it works, why change it? Why change our hermetically sealed environment, which we've equipped with our favorite food, music, and temperature controls? Our ego-bubble becomes stronger and stronger as it tries to protect what we've acquired. It expends tremendous energy maintaining itself, not letting in anything new. And because this process denies the reality of change, it also denies us the opportunity to truly contact our experience.

"WASH ME, BUT DON'T GET ME WET"

There's a German expression that says, "Wash me, but don't get me wet." When we encounter something that might touch us, change our belief, or shift our perception a little, we develop a stress reaction, close our hearts and minds, and leave the scene. We have many ways of leaving: overeating, working out, watching TV, becoming angry or depressed. Any return to the superfamiliar will do.

We retreat into habitual patterns because they seem solid and comforting. We might even regard them as our power. However, because we see this power as coming from our own resources (which are finite), not from something greater, we have to work hard to maintain them, for the inner power might run out. This leads to more stress. We want to fit into a space-time continuum what does not fit in that continuum. We want to dance in many marriages at the same time—undertake many activities at once. We're so busy at this that we hardly breathe. We hardly take the time to focus our energy field in our life.

We identify with our small, habitual patterns instead of with the greater space that we are. When we restrict our perception in this way, true relationship—from which health, peace, and healing energy spring—cannot occur. We wind ourselves tighter. This tension crystallizes into mental, physical, and spiritual "identities"—closed systems of habitual energy patterns that cause us more pain.

"Fixing" ourselves in this matrix and projecting it onto others and the world leads to mental, physical, and spiritual disease—individual and collective. Death, decay, degradation, dominance, and control come from resisting our own expansive nature. Through the stress that the resistance creates, our consciousness crystallizes; even on the physical level our patterns of rigidity—arthritis, atherosclerosis—manifest.

NORMALITY—OR ARRESTED DEVELOPMENT?

Culturally, there is little incentive to practice living from essential identity. Indeed, there is heavy pressure to be "someone," to achieve something, combined with a bombardment of heart-numbing stimuli. No wonder we forget who we are.

We make an intellectual judgment about everything that enters our field, and we stay with it. That is the definition of "normality." My definition of normality is arrested development. We're in it together. Our collective fog becomes the distorted lens through which we see ourselves, our world, and each other. It is a conspiracy to fall asleep and to stay asleep, ignorant of innate human dignity, true wealth, and true medicine.

Luckily, it works the other way around, too. Any effort that any one of us makes to wake up affects everyone else.

The materialism of the small world is clearly necessary. Someone has to make the money, take care of the children, plant the crops, and cook the food. All these activities require careful tending of the "outer." But the small story becomes problematic when we become stuck in it. We identify with it and believe that's all there is. We forget the "inner."

Integrating the Big and Small

Both sides—the person of the world, and the man or woman of spirit—must become integrated. When we be-

gin to see ourselves as an eternal life force—a very mysterious one—that is for now operating in a human body,
we're able to surrender and miracles happen. Miracles are
waiting for us to look up from our third-dimensional,
small-story identification, from our belief that our imaginary bubble of survival is all that there is.

A few years ago I met His Holiness the Dalai Lama, the
spiritual and political leader of Tibet, when we were both
keynote speakers at the Congress of Holistic Medicine in
Bangalore, India. I was traveling with my wife, my three-
month-old daughter, and some friends. The day after the
opening ceremony, I had been meditating in my hotel
room and suddenly felt an urge to put on my jogging
shoes and get some fresh air. As I left the hotel, there was
His Holiness. We went for a long walk together, and I felt
a very strong connection with him. After our walk he
invited me to visit him in Dharamsala, where he lives in
exile. I was delighted to accept.

After touring southern India, where we explored
Ayurvedic medical centers, we flew to Jamu in Kashmir.
There we were met by a jeep that had been sent by His
Holiness. Five hours and three flat tires later I found myself sitting in his living room, discussing his tradition's
concepts of the "daily self" and the "subtle self." We
clearly defined the "daily self" as the "actor," the one
who carries out actions, literally, in the small world. The
daily self works, eats, plays, disciplines the children, sets
up the family budget, takes in the car for maintenance,
and does all the other actions we can observe with our
five senses.

While we were discussing these interactions with the
daily self, I suddenly sensed the continuity behind all
those actions. In that moment I had a feeling of having
always been, that there was some vital, essential part of

myself that wasn't supported by what I did. I looked into the eyes of His Holiness. He was smiling at me.

"This subtle self that I felt—that we've always been . . ." I stammered.

The Dalai Lama nodded and said, "Of course."

I felt my sense of self elongating, encompassing everything in my life, and stretching out even beyond my life. I told him, "There is no beginning and no end."

The Dalai Lama continued to smile and said, "Nor birth, nor death."

"No alpha, and no omega," I continued.

Then we looked deep into each other's eyes and started laughing.

We laughed because the realization of one's essential identity is a liberating and healing experience. And it's very simple. The transformative and healing power of our essential identity is amazingly strong. Prejudices, limitations, and fear of death are altered so thoroughly by this state of awareness that we may become driven to try to make it our residence of choice. It takes a lot of time and change to even contact this expanded, accepting identity, and even more to make it our predominant one.

The path of mastery begins with remembering that we are an infinite mystery. We can then start to wake up— turn on a little light and move forward. The first place we need to shine this light of awareness is on our own makeup.

I was first an M.D. and then a psychiatrist and then I pursued spirituality. I looked in the mirror one day and asked, "What makes me think I can be a doctor and practice medicine when I don't know anything except science?" Science was not enough for me because I had learned about it *out there*, not within. It can be easy to study and become the best student. You just have to entrain your energy with the professor's and nod all the time, be a yes man.

"Eleven years of college learning and university medical training," I thought, "does not give me what I need to deal with other people's lives. It's a big responsibility." So I became a *fakir*—which in the Sufi tradition means "poor"—because it occurred to me that God knew everything and I knew just what I had learned in books. I gave away all my possessions and went to Morocco, where I lived on an estate with sixty other men who were also learning to surrender. Our daily routine centered around rituals dedicated to self-discovery and the science of service. For eleven months I prayed, meditated, and studied the teachings of Sufism. Each morning began with the chant, "There is no God but reality. There is no reality but God." Even the chores we did every day after lunch (I usually picked fruit in the courtyard) were considered part of our devotions—not an interruption. As my teacher Hassan said, "Manual labor is an extension of God's work in this world."

Then things shifted; for the last twenty years I've been talking to people, telling them that life is precious and sacred. This message is not new, it is *now*. It is not New Age, it is eternal. Only when I turned my attention to becoming "spiritual" did I realize that I had been pursuing a spiritual path from the beginning. We all are—not in order to become spiritual people, or worldly people, but in order to become human beings.

Becoming human involves learning to align ourselves with our hearts—with heaven, earth, and the elements in a unified field, which is what is generated by divine energy. I think we're ripe enough to be human. We may be so ripe we're almost rotten!

As a physician, I have seen that healing the connection to essence and the infinite intelligence of the universe by opening our hearts reactivates the capacity for self-repair that goes from the cell to the cosmos. We are all interconnected. For example, the process of reading the words in this book is the result of more elements than we ordinarily imagine. The trees from which the paper is made grew because there was sunlight, moisture, and soil to sustain them. Someone cut the trees and trucked them to the mill to begin their long journey into paperhood. Others were involved in calling the book into being and shaping the words that you are reading now. Someone else manufactured the ink. Designers and typesetters, printers and binders, crafted the paper and the words into form. Truckdrivers drove the book to the bookstores; clerks put it on the shelf; people at the bank maintained your account so that money was there for you to buy it. By the same token, someone designed and built the chair that you are sitting in as you now read.

We speak of "codependence" as if it is something to avoid, yet even the simplest transaction—buying food at the grocery store, for example—is an intricate marvel of codependence. We are all interconnected.

Modern medicine is also finally beginning to acknowledge the interconnectedness from which we all spring. For example, Larry Dossey, an M.D. who has pioneered studies of the power of prayer in healing, has recently defined the current trend in medicine as "Era III," which (as opposed to the mechanistic medicine of "Era I" and the mind-body medicine of "Era II") recognizes that healing is by nature nonlocal and transpersonal. Not lodged in space and time, through imagery, prayer, and other nonlocal methods, the power of healing extends through space and time to affect distant bodies. The power of healing is love. Era III medicine rests in the knowledge that we are all part of a global mind network. The work of Andrew Weil, M.D., is an example of the balance of allopathic and natural medicine and its application to optimum health.

The more of us who can open our hearts to give and receive the energy of the universe, the more healing will occur on every level. None of us is isolated. Living in tune with the higher aspiration is what motivates this work. Living and healing from essence is much bigger than most healing paradigms. It involves awakening to a greater essential life, the journey of the soul.

Essence is. It is the mere existence of the eternal majesty of itself. What would our lives be like if we treated ourselves as who we are instead of looking for our soul, afraid that if we don't behave well our soul will be taken from us?

And how would life look on planet earth if we could construct a society of souls instead of a society of bodies? If you and I acknowledge that we embody the majestic, eternal force of life, won't we relate, legislate, educate, medicate, copulate, and so on differently than we do now? Undoubtedly so. We would treat each other with care.

Care does not happen in the frequency of the head. Care happens in the frequency of the heart.

This paradigm shift from head to heart, from information to essence, is not new for humanity. We started out with a hunter-gatherer identity. That changed to an agricultural identity. That shifted in the nineteenth century to an industrial identity. The paradigms of the twentieth century thus far have shifted us to a social identity, then to an informational identity. We are still transforming our consciousness to higher and higher levels of perception.

Perhaps the twenty-first century will bring the age in which we stop identifying with the last of our false veils and live from the peaceful, joyous, nondualistic, nonjudgmental space of our essential identity.

❂ **EXERCISE** ❂
CELEBRATING OURSELVES AS LIGHT

The energy of essence is light. As essence, the core of our being is ineffable golden light.

Visualize a magnificent glowing ball of golden light. Make this golden ball as big as you can in your imagination.

Now visualize millions of rays of light shooting out from the giant ball. Imagine the vast brilliance spreading throughout space. Now visualize one of the incredibly bright rays coming to rest in your heart.

Visualize yourself, wherever you are, carrying this light-ray in your heart, and at the same time see that pieces of the greater ball of light have also landed in the sun, stars, moon, and other heavenly bodies.

Each of these aspects of the one essence are now on an incredible journey throughout the universe, traveling further and further from that original source, but all contain a celebration of light.

Imagine yourself traveling far, far away through the universe. Now look down and see the other particles of light in the heavens below. Look up and see the particles of light in the heavens above. Look around and see that particles of light surround you. Come back to your body by projecting the light-wave outside yourself and riding it to earth, knowing that all heavenly bodies are connected by this light.

Now visualize yourself on earth. Imagine yourself surrounded by other people, who are also projecting particles of light from their hearts.

Relax, and rest in the remembrance of being a luminous particle of interconnected totality, a unit of consciousness holographically occurring.

CHAPTER FOUR

———————— ❖ ————————

You Aren't Who You *Think* You Are

Recovering the sacred is the direction of the Buddhist tradition, the Christian tradition, the Sufi tradition, the shamanistic tradition, the Hindu tradition, and the Jewish tradition. But recovering the sacred is not the direction of the postindustrial age at the end of the twentieth century.

I have a prayer that goes like this:

> Oh Lord, please quickly make disappear that which is not real. Make the bubbles that we create to protect and keep ourselves in the third-dimensional, small-story world hurry up and pop, instead of hanging around just because they worked the last time we needed them and we think they'll work again. I pledge to uphold the highest good for all.

In this prayer we're asking for what is larger than ourselves, larger than our bubble, to make disappear *fast* what is not real. This is a prayer from the heart.

By turning ourselves away from the singular mind of the small story (the third and fourth dimensions of awareness) to the universal mind of the big story (the fifth dimension of awareness and beyond) we are saying, "Thy will be done." We are acknowledging that the will of the highest aspiration—our personal aspiration, the collective aspiration, the aspiration of divine energy—can cut through, destroy, evaporate, disintegrate, dissolve the false boundary that has us believing that we exist separately from the universal ocean of life.

The false boundary is called temporary identity. It is the result of living in our heads. The path of the head is what we travel in the small story of the third dimension.

Why Do We Forget Essence?

In the process of development, the essence that we are tends to get overshadowed by false identification. That's okay for the purpose of learning third-dimensional techniques. It is good for a baby to be physically conscious when beginning to walk. It is good for a teenager who starts to discriminate to be emotionally aware. It is wonderful for a person who is designing a career, a life, or a service to be intellectually conscious.

However, when we believe that we *are* our bodies, that we *are* our emotions, or that we *are* our minds, that is not all right. Then we are clearly on the third-dimensional road to the three D's: decay, degradation, and death.

This road is a good place to wake up. Seeing old age, sickness, and death is exactly what woke up the Buddha. When he was still a royal prince (Prince Siddhartha), the Buddha found out that three-D existence was the opposite of eternal truth. Even though his father, the king, had sheltered him in a glorious hothouse environment of

pleasure—food and drink, sport and comfort, even dancing girls—one day Prince Siddhartha ventured into the
world beyond the palace and was shocked by what he
saw. What he saw was fairly simple, although even in our
own time we are still somewhat protected from it. Along
the roadside he saw a sick person, an extremely old person, and a dying person. He was shocked at the contrast
between life on the outside and his protected existence
inside the palace. That very day he left his father, wife,
and infant son; his comfort, pleasure, and entertainment;
his legacy as prince. Drawn away by the inescapable reality of life, he set out without any royal trappings to anchor himself in the truth of the eternal. He left his father's
palace to discover his essential identity. He set out to
recover the sacred.

When we know ourselves as essence, we say, "I am."
This is a fifth-dimensional realization. Before we know
ourselves as essence, we say, "I am this; I am that." These
are third- and fourth-dimensional statements. Once we
define ourselves as being "this" or "that" we have to fight
to protect this or that. Such a process is inherently stressful. Most of our life force goes into defending the false
identity that we have learned to accept as ourselves.

The Nafs

Early in our lives we adopt what in the Sufi tradition are
called *nafs,* or false personalities, temporary identities. A
nafs is a third-dimensional identification, the means by
which we function in this world. Nafs are not what we
Westerners call masks or personae; rather, they are the
conditioned responses of the soul. Once our soul takes
on these identities, these soul-energized "selves" are the

nafs. These subpersonalities tend to crystallize as the whole; unless we embark on a spiritual journey, we are likely to regard them as ourselves.

In order not to take these parts as our whole, we must learn positive core values. Learning to identify with core virtues is absolutely necessary. Otherwise, instead of identifying with essence, we will regard confused and often conflicted nafs as "our" mind.

Nafs are not inherently bad. There are instinctual-animal-self nafs, intellectual nafs, emotional nafs. There are nafs of all kinds. They are the vehicles of essence. If we don't devote ourselves to continuous inner work, they are like horses going in all directions at once.

But if we are committed to our essential journey and work to develop ourselves from within, our temporary identities eventually reflect our essence. The nafs become stabilized and integrated. If we are able to stabilize our identity beyond the nafs, then the true human mind—the treasure that lies hidden and incipient within each of us—is awakened.

This is where a teacher often comes into the picture. I personally had the good fortune of studying with Idries Shah, the renowned Sufi teacher who died in 1996. Far from being old-fashioned, anachronistic, or full of mumbo-jumbo, the teaching I received from him was a synthesis of enlightened and progressive investigations that have allowed me to go beyond organized religion and belief systems in order to recognize essence in myself and others.

As embodied essence, we move in and out of temporary identities all the time. We all adopt and maintain temporary identities, taking on different ones at different times in our lives—even at different times in our days.

There is nothing wrong with this. It is necessary action to survive in a social world.

It is natural and healthy to invest ourselves in a naf, the Sufis say, as long as we do it with a sense of surrender and detachment. When we have big-story vision, we can move into the appropriate role when necessary and leave it when we need to do something else, or when it's no longer useful. But we don't want the nafs to acquire a life of its own.

Nafs become a problem when we forget that we are essence. Then we tend to *solidify* them and use them as an unnecessary reference point. We become attached to them. Our self-esteem depends on them. We weave them together to make a solid "me."

When you wake up in the morning, you may be in the nafs of spouse or lover (or zombie, if you aren't a morning person). Then someone calls from work and you switch to your professional nafs. Then your mother calls with some advice and you switch into your adult child nafs. Then the kids aren't dressed for school, so you switch to your parent nafs. You've already gone through four nafs even before you've had your shower or your morning coffee. Through the course of the day you might also be a driver, a meditator, a cook, a soccer player, and so on. These nafs, however, can present problems, particularly if we see them as solid rather than fluid.

These are called *outer identities*. We identify with our appearance, with what we do in order to make money, with our family or relationship. "I'm a beautiful woman." "I'm a doctor." "I'm a mother." "I'm a spiritual person." Each of these roles is an expression of the self that is multidimensionally journeying through universes in order to experience the ALL of divine energy. When we are temporarily identified with any of these roles, we don't see that they are merely impermanent manifestations. We think they constitute our *self*. To identify with them in a solid way is to obscure the fluidity of essence. It's as if we hold ourselves in one role, whatever it may be, instead of allowing ourselves to move unencumbered through space as the light beings that we are. When we allow ourselves this liberation, we become as flexible as bamboo in the wind. No longer do we hold ourselves frozen in defense against any change that might arise.

Psychological identities or inner identities can be as riveting as expressions anchored in profession, appearance, or family.

For example, a disheveled, anxious-looking woman came into my clinic when I was living in Colorado years ago. She had been referred to me by another doctor.

"How can I help you?" I asked.

With hardly a pause the woman breathlessly replied, "I'm a paranoid-schizophrenic alcoholic."

I was taken aback. As I looked at her in amazement, I responded, "But aren't you still a human being?"

"Still?" She pondered for a moment. Then, "You're right. I guess I'd forgotten that."

Labels like "paranoid-schizophrenic," "addict," or even "upwardly mobile" are useful in defining a complex set of motivations and behaviors. Sometimes, however, we identify ourselves or others so strongly with the label that we don't allow for change or growth. For example, although the woman who came into my office had abstained from alcohol for over three years, she was still calling herself an alcoholic. Although such identification is encouraged by Alcoholics Anonymous, I prefer to call it "expressing the nafs of drinking alcohol." In this way, we do not tie our identity to a diagnosis.

Was it possible that this woman could start drinking again? Of course. But the identification with her *past* life and her *future* potential to abuse alcohol was obscuring her *present* life, where she was an ordinary human being, essence personified.

THE NAFS OF ADDICTION

Addictions are a particularly subtle form of false identity, or nafs. The addiction could be as lethal as heroin or as seemingly benign as a story line—an internal narrative that we tell ourselves over and over again. In any case, what the addiction gives us is a materialistic way to connect with our memory of the nondualistic fifth-dimensional energy of essence.

Addiction can be comforting because, through its sheerly repetitive nature, it relaxes our ego-bubble. As anyone who smokes, drinks, abuses drugs, overeats, plays video games, or shops to excess knows, addictive activity mesmerizes and comforts us. It has the quality of a lullaby. We lose ourselves in the memory of essence, a floating (and fleeting, when it's substance-induced) feeling of oneness with the universe. What we are seeking is love.

However, as the song says, we're looking for love in all the wrong places. With addictive behavior we draw a small, tight circle around ourselves. This lets us escape into a tiny realm that is defined by need and desire. When the world at large becomes too big and too frightening, addictive behavior decreases the world's size to the satisfaction of a smoke, a drink, an enormous meal, new clothes—whatever gives us the illusion of being in control.

Addiction is a peculiar third-dimensional path in which

we connect with *substances* rather than *essence*. In the 1960s, for example, it was quite common for people who had peak experiences on mind-altering drugs to then pursue the drugs instead of their expanding awareness.

Recently I read about a new television channel devoted to recovering from addictive behavior. It occurred to me that the nafs of addiction in our culture has taken on the stature of religious identity, but somewhat in reverse. When we identify with a religion, we tend to identify with a power greater than ourselves. But as addicts we identify with a smaller power. Identifying ourselves as addicts is a way of shrinking our realm of experience to a tiny pinpoint, the center of which is "poor me" who cannot make it through the day without, without, without . . . whatever it is that makes my world small enough for me to deal with it. As addicts we always have something to lean on if the world becomes too much for us to handle. We abdicate responsibility and give it to the nafs. Sooner or later we have shrunk not only our world but also our sense of ourselves, into whatever substance or activity we allow to control us.

Addictions do not occur only in the form of substances or external activities; we can also be addicted to thought forms, energies, or channeling entities of a fourth-dimensional nature, such as angels or other spirits. In many cases of addiction I have worked with an exorcism technique to restore the deeper strength of the "addict." I encourage the "addict" to visualize himself or herself in a tunnel of light, cutting the strings to the addiction and tying them off with affirmations and bright light. This restores a stronger sense of the core self.

THE NAFS OF VICTIM

"Victim" is an ultracharged, false identification because of the anger and powerlessness that are likely to accompany it, often combined with a healthy case of "If only . . .": "If only I hadn't walked down that street," "If only I hadn't pushed so hard," "If only I hadn't been going so fast." All these statements arise from our belief that we have control over everything that happens to us. Oddly enough, when something good comes to us unexpectedly, we are likely to attribute it to ineffable factors such as synchronicity and luck. What it all comes down to is that we often have no control, and there are also times when we have no choice. What life dishes out is not always up to us.

However, how we *deal with* what life dishes out is up to us. Whether our situation is heaven or hell depends on our perception. If we keep our contracted awareness focused on what happened, our world will get pretty small. If we're able to find a way to accept what happens to us, process it, and move on, we're less likely to dwell in the identity of victim. Forgiving ourselves and others can be an important part of the inner work involved.

One example of true victimization is the people who survived the Holocaust. However, the outcome was different for people like Victor Frankl, Elie Wiesel, and others who kept their inner core intact. Rather than withering inside, they used their Holocaust experiences to nourish their inner strength and pass it along to others, in service or in teaching.

A paraplegic woman in her mid-thirties named Carol came to me recently for help with depression and marital discord. Two years earlier she had been left paralyzed by a car accident. The fears, worries, and discontent that she brought up in our sessions were affecting her marriage, which had been healthy before the accident. Although they sounded reasonable, it seemed to me that everything she was saying led back to a "victim" identity.

"If you will allow it to happen," I told her, "something in this experience is leading you toward greater awareness of your essential self. First, can you forgive yourself for being in that car accident? There was nothing you could have done to prevent it. It was a rainy night, visibility was bad, and you did all you could to avoid the accident."

Carol's anger at herself gradually dissipated over the next several sessions. At the same time, her contempt for the driver who had crashed into her car grew and grew. "How can I ever forgive something like that?" she demanded. The way she tried to shift her body in her wheelchair was a reminder of the heaviness, inertia, and helplessness that she seemed to feel.

"Your future happiness and health depend on your ability to forgive him," I said. I explained how her hatred for the driver of the other car was a stressful inner energy that would, if unreleased, slowly contribute to the deterioration of her body.

I had recently realized that I, as a Jewish person, had let myself remain an indirect victim of the Holocaust by not forgiving Adolf Hitler for his crimes against the Jewish people. As a result, I had often been defensive when issues about religion and ethnic identity came up.

I used my recent insight as an illustration for Carol.

"How can you forgive someone as evil as Hitler?" she asked. "After all he did?"

I leaned back and smiled. "Forgiving Hitler doesn't mean that I think what he did was all right," I told her. "I can recognize that he was following his own misguided,

and in my view, evil, path, which led to incalculable suffering. However, he is dead now. Forgiving him means
that it's high time I release the negative energy I have
been harboring. That energy is not hurting him or aveng-
ing my relations whom he killed. On the contrary, that
energy is hurting only me—destroying me, in fact."

Awareness of her "victim" identity combined with forgiveness opened up my patient's life. Now she is com-
bining trips to her neurologist with Chi Kung and
acupuncture treatments. She is much more relaxed and
accepting of her physical condition. Releasing her solidly
held view of herself as "victim" has also helped her family and friends. She realized they had gone beyond supporting her to reinforcing and enabling her victim
identity.

THE NAFS OF ENABLER

In situations like Carol's, those around the "victim" can
easily manifest the identity of "enabler" simply by trying
to help. In an effort to express their care, they end up
treating as an object the person they are trying to support.
They focus on the river that separates them from their
loved one, instead of on the bridge they could make.
That kind of caring is called sympathy. It is rooted in a
concept. We look across the river at an object and feel
pity. "Oh, you poor thing!" and "You'd better take it
easy!" and "Let me do that for you!" in fact solidify the
temporary identity of victim as the enabler also begins to
falsely identify with his or her role in the situation. It
rarely leads to positive action, because it tends to "freeze"
the victim in that role. We tend to do this because we find
the victim's situation threatening. Offering to help him
stay in his identity as victim is a way of saying, in effect,

"This happened to you, but it could never happen to me." The gulf between us widens. As we enforce his victimhood, we enforce our own denial.

When we operate from an interdimensional viewpoint, however, our ability to connect with the open energies of the fourth and fifth dimensions allows us to move beyond the closed system of temporary identification. In the enabler nafs, for example, we can connect with the fourth-dimensional state of compassion, which in turn may lead us to the fifth-dimensional state of empathy. Compassion and empathy are bridging qualities. No longer do we focus on the imaginary river flowing between us and the "victim." We do not feel threatened by what happened to him, but acknowledge that "there but for the grace of God go I." With compassion and empathy, we become a bridge. We recognize that true caring involves helping others move on with their lives in productive, fulfilling ways. From higher states of awareness, then, we would say things like, "I know that you're going through a very difficult period right now, and when you feel ready, I'd like to help you build a new life."

THE NAFS OF STORY LINES

A very subtle, inner, and false identification happens when we solidify beliefs about ourselves and the world around us into story lines. Story lines are made of misperceptions, fear, self-doubt, opinion, past conditioning, prejudices, and assumptions. They are conclusions we have drawn about ourselves and the world. They may have been appropriate conclusions at one time in our lives, but when we weave them into a seamless world view they can be confining.

Story lines can have underlying themes of fear and

anxiety, judgment and criticism, depression, arrogance, self-belittlement, or complaining. They tend to be self-fulfilling, which reinforces our identification with them. Here are some examples of stories that we might tell ourselves over and over again:

"I'm not good enough; there's something wrong with me; I'm unworthy and undeserving."

"Life is painful; it is not meant to be fun."

"Mother was right. I can't do anything well. I'll never amount to anything."

"Money is the root of all evil; money corrupts; I must not allow it into my life."

"I don't have any control over what happens to me; I'm powerless to do anything about my life or the state of the world."

"Other people's needs are more important than mine; it's a sin to pay attention to my own needs."

"Love is dangerous; I'll get hurt; it's not worth it."

"Power is bad; if I claim my power, I will hurt someone; I must deny and hide my power."

"Women don't show their anger; I'm a woman; therefore I must be nice even though I'm furious."

"Only sissies cry. I'm not a sissy. Therefore I'd better not show my feelings."

When we identify with story lines, we may come to associate our inner lives with a steady stream of self-absorbed thoughts that are fixated on our behavior and appearance in the outer world.

We all have particular habitual thought patterns, beliefs, and assumptions that make up our story lines. What are yours? Write them down to help increase your awareness of them, which removes some of their solidity and power. When we recognize the stories we tell ourselves, we're able to change them into positive thoughts and affirmations, which are useful tools for expanding our awareness of ourselves as essence.

We also have temporary identities as a culture, and as a culture we tend to solidify them. Three of the more prevalent nafs of Western culture today are that of "progress," that of "science," and that of "New Age spirituality."

THE NAFS OF PROGRESS

The nafs of progress has us conditioned to believe that we can expect to become better and better. We can expect less pain, more pleasure, and overall happiness. All our investments should grow at an accelerated rate. The nafs of progress is based on identifying with outer conditions. We identify with human doing instead of human being.

The goals of the material plane are relatively simple: survive, leave children to survive, have some comfort and dignity. As soon as our basic survival needs are met, we expect to rest in contentment. But we don't. New, less basic needs arise and our sense of contentment ebbs. I call this complicating simplicity, and our advertising- and consumer-driven culture actively encourages it. For example, rather than relax with our comfortable old furnishings, we are encouraged to redecorate so that everything matches. If we do this, we'll find ourselves in an environment where we're protecting the furniture, the carpets, the curtains, and the walls from scratches and dirt. Then our home is no longer comfortable, not even for the dog.

Or we've put aside enough money for our children to attend the state university, but by the time they're in junior high school we decide—based on our own feelings, not on our children's proclivities—that it isn't enough. We feel inadequate that we can't pay for an Ivy League school, so we spend the next few years working like mad in order to fulfill our increased expectations. We never even see our children anymore; we're too busy. Our minds run wild as we raise our standards, and we stress out under higher expectations. By the same token, if we are sick or unhappy we are likely to believe that something from outside ourselves will make us well or content.

THE NAFS OF SCIENCE

The nafs of science has conditioned us to believe that the material dimension bound by time and space is the only dimension that exists, that we live in a dead world where everything—including ourselves—is matter in lifeless space. Science, for all its beneficial qualities, has introduced us to an illusory objective reality, and most of us measure ourselves against it. In doing this we learn to deny our own experience. It's as if we are constantly trying to incorporate everyday life into a barrage of statistics. Our own perception falters against the scientific view of "how things are." We believe that everything can be explained. Our conditioning leads us to disregard the mystery of life until we run head-first against it in the form of birth, death, and love. It is heartening that even science has moved beyond its mechanistic belief system and into a more mystical view of reality, as evidenced by quantum physics. As scientists have continued to break down the universe into quantifiable parts, they've discovered that some parts are not quantifiable and do not follow the rules. Thus, the latter part of the twentieth century has seen the introduction of black holes and chaos theory. Yet as Chögyam Trungpa, a Tibetan Buddhist teacher who helped bring those teachings to the West, expressed it, "Chaos should be regarded as extremely good news."

Because science studies material processes, it tends to deny the existence of what can't be seen and proved. This nafs denies greater dimensions of awareness such as prayer and telepathy, which can't be documented and measured.

If we have accepted this nafs, we are likely to feel that if we can't prove our inner experience, it doesn't exist. For example, my students always seem to be asking, "You know, I had this wonderful experience; do you think it's real?" Indeed, many of us are conditioned to doubt the magic of our own perception.

THE NAFS OF NEW AGE SPIRITUALITY

A lot of New Age spirituality is the rote repetition of healing and other spiritual techniques that are not tailor-made and prescribed for the individual. It's the franchising of spirituality.

Once upon a time there was a teacher and a disciple. The disciple asked the teacher to give him a prayer, a meditation. The master gave him a sentence to repeat: "Is it worth it?"

To remind himself of his practice, the student wrote on a slip of paper, "The master says continually to ask yourself the question, 'Is it worth it?' " Then he went to a diner and contemplated his question while he ate.

When he went to pay the check, he accidentally left the slip of paper on the table. But since he'd already learned it by heart, he didn't need it anymore.

Now a woman sat down at the same table and saw this slip of paper. She read it, took it to heart, and went home. Her children greeted her with, "Mommy, Mommy, feed me, I'm hungry." She said, "Is it worth it?" So she didn't feed her children. Her husband came home, saw what was happening, and they had a big fight.

Back at the diner, the paper remained on the table. A beautiful young woman came in and read it. When she got home, her boyfriend came over with a diamond ring and said, "Beloved, would you marry me?" She replied, "Is it worth it?" The boyfriend left, disappointed, taking the diamond ring with him; that was the end of their relationship.

Then came a soldier. He saw this slip of paper, "Is it worth it?" He went back to the king's palace, where he was a guard. The enemies were coming and his general said, "Close the gates!" The soldier replied, "Is it worth it?" He was court-martialed and beheaded.

What everyone was repeating was a prescription for the first person, who had left the piece of paper on the table. Everyone was willing to follow this instruction, even though it wasn't for them, because they were asleep to themselves.

In the sleep-state created by solidifying temporary identities, we can be so focused on what comes from *outside* that we forget to remember who we really are and how we can connect to divine healing energy. When we identify with the so-called New Age, we draw another little circle around ourselves—perhaps delineated by planetary movements, a passing comet, the last workshop we attended, or our politically and ecologically correct behavior. Our adopted identity then acts as an obstacle to discovering our own inner truth.

Going Beyond Nafs

There are two important aspects of getting beyond our nafs. It requires a constitutional change in (1) who we think we are, and (2) how we express ourselves in attitude and activity.

First, through giving ourselves over to the present moment we develop the ability to remember who we are. We open our hearts to essence.

Second, by cultivating our inner awareness we will develop the ability to see our inner world moment-by-moment. With the aspiration to do this, each of us has unique individual efforts and creativity from which to draw. Working with ourselves in any way that works, we can learn how to take responsibility for our inner life. This is an empowering and healing path.

Three Skills for Decrystallizing Solidified Nafs

When we surrender to heaven and earth we are giving ourselves the opportunity to cultivate three skills that actively decrystallize confining temporary identities—be they emotional, physical, or spiritual. These three skills have the power to automatically introduce us to the workings of our inner world. As we cultivate them, we will physically experience *lightheartedness;* these three skills physically lighten our hearts. They are (1) observing without judgment, (2) accepting what is happening, and (3) letting go.

As we develop the ability to apply these qualities inside, we gain the ability to do it outside as well. We can let go of ego judgments long enough to see ourselves and others more clearly, accepting ourselves and others as we are, right here, in this moment.

OBSERVING WITHOUT JUDGMENT

Pure awareness comes from essence. Usually, however, when we tune in to our minds, what we experience is the "little mind" of ego. This is the path of the head. Buddhist teachers have called it monkey-mind. It's the little voice inside our heads that swings from thought to thought, constantly judging and commenting on our experiences. It is particularly entwined with the nafs of the story line. It tricks us into tuning in to our story line instead of what's actually happening. Yet behind our story line is the pure awareness of essence.

Remaining present with what *is* allows us to open to whatever arises in our world and remain at peace. If we commit ourselves to this practice, we discover that we have the power to boycott our usual reactive defenses. We remain clear, our inner eyes wide open, simply observing without judgment. We are aligning ourselves with the path of heart.

This is a way to cultivate inner space, through which awareness dawns. Through continued practice, we learn how to maintain our connections with this level of awareness. We become more aware of the tricks that our monkey-mind plays on us with judgments and story lines. We don't try to get rid of that little voice, but we do learn to notice it and refocus our awareness. This is how we begin to avoid succumbing to the whirlpool-like energy of story lines. We learn that when we get pulled into habitual patterns, our vision narrows and we shut down.

Nonjudgmental observation widens our vision. We no longer automatically label or define everything. We begin to observe things as they are, from inner stillness. We can recognize thoughts as thoughts. From the stillness of essence, we simply observe them and let them pass on by.

ACCEPTING

Fully accepting—without judgment—what each moment offers allows us to open more completely. For example, if you have a toothache, you can label what you feel as "pain" rather than extend the simple sensation of discomfort to include anxiety about a root canal, your fear of the dentist, your lack of dental insurance, and other thoughts. Returning to "pain" or any other perception effectively cuts through the pyramid of thought patterns we habitually build on top of it.

When we simply notice what is happening without embellishment, we're not blinded to it by our past associations with similar events. We have fresh eyes. Rather than avoiding or escaping unpleasant or distressing events, we're able to live with them and become curious about them. Seeing with fresh eyes, we're willing to experience pain or pleasure as it is, uncolored by thoughts and assumptions. We see thoughts as thoughts, emotions as emotions, pain as pain, pleasure as pleasure. Accepting what arises as it is allows us to experience it fully.

Instead of judging the events in our lives as good, bad, right, or wrong, we now begin to recognize that nothing is good or bad in and of itself, and that everything represents something from which we can benefit. This does not mean that we have to like everything that happens. It simply means that when we remain open even to our adversities and accept them for what they are, we may find within them an energy that allows us to move forward. Now each situation we encounter offers us the precious opportunity of using it to open our hearts further by cultivating positive feelings.

LETTING GO

Reconnecting with heart allows us to develop another important capacity: the ability to let go. Like the caterpillar and the butterfly, if we are going to become who we truly are, we are going to have to let go of our old, limiting identities. There comes a time when we outgrow our cocoons and must leave them behind. This can be frightening because we want to hold on to the familiar, even when it becomes painful. Yet when awakened, the quiet voice of our heart urges us to let go so that we can fly forward.

Practices of inner awareness (such as opening our senses to heaven and earth, meditation, deep relaxation, and psychological modeling) give us the chance to experience letting go of self-defeating and stress-producing thoughts, emotions, and physical sensations. Whenever we release any of these limiting perceptions or distorted beliefs, we are releasing our old attachments. Our awareness expands to include who we are at the level of essence. The caterpillar matures into the butterfly, and we find the freedom that we have been seeking.

When we objectify ourselves, others, and everything around us and then identify with our objects (for example, money in the bank, relationships, professions, internal or external states of any kind), we become dependent on and attached to objects outside ourselves. Without them, we're nothing. We can spend our entire lives jumping from one object to another. We find ourselves asking, "Is this all there is?"

Because life in the dimension of time and space is characterized by impermanence, circumstances change all the time. When the objects with which we have identified change, we feel vulnerable. When we feel very vulnerable, illness can occur. Then we look for another object to "cure" us.

On the other hand, when we are not identified with objects in the third dimension, we identify with subject—our essential self, not the "me" that's woven into place with temporary identities. When we identify with something bigger than "me," our awareness expands. We begin to be able to see first our reactions to threatening circumstances, and then the mechanisms that cause these reactions. This is fourth-dimensional awareness.

Our expanding awareness ultimately leads to the discovery of our essential self, which is beyond space and time. Here we are not susceptible to the loss and gain, the hope of pleasure and fear of pain, that rules everything outside us. We are not attached to the objects of the present that cause suffering; instead we begin to resonate with the essential self, which is untouched by suffering. This is the expanded awareness of the fifth dimension.

Healing Identities

Given all the ways it's possible to identify ourselves falsely with something "outer," it's hardly surprising that we can solidify our identification with healing modalities. In the past fifteen years or so as our awareness of alternative therapies in particular has expanded exponentially, debate has raged as to the effectiveness or "rightness" of one modality over another.

Thus, people who are trained in the field of allopathic medicine champion clinically tested methods such as chemotherapy and radiation, whereas others rush to "prove" the effectiveness of alternative therapies such as homeopathy and acupuncture. New Age or spiritual types look down their noses at pharmacological treatments such as Prozac, whereas people who have a more scientific perspective question the efficacy of prayer and meditation. The debate over healing methodology obscures larger issues: (1) that there may be no one "right" treatment, and (2) that a connection with essence is a strong component of true healing.

When we *identify* with an "outer" therapy that we think will make us well, we invest in it a great deal of hope and fear. Identifying with the technique closes us to our inner healing power, which is our connection with essence. A conceptual identification can also blind us to our situation.

A pregnant woman and her husband, strong "believers" in alternative medicine and extremely distrustful of allopathic methods, were determined to have their baby at home. One morning three weeks before the baby was due, the woman awoke with a high fever. Her midwife advised her to go to the hospital; fearing the worst, she finally did, giving up her dream of a holistic birth experience for her child. When she arrived at the hospital she was advised to start a round of antibiotics immediately, which she refused. She then went into labor.

Because of her high fever and the fact that the baby

seemed to be in stress, the doctors wanted to puncture the amniotic sac so that the baby could be born. The woman and her husband refused. They were still determined to have a home birth. When their midwife arrived at the hospital hours later, she urged them to follow the doctor's advice. When the water was broken, it was full of meconium—the baby's fecal matter—a sign of extreme stress. The baby was delivered by emergency Caesarean section and died fourteen hours later.

When we are acting from a centered place—the open heart—we can go beyond concept in choosing the appropriate tool. We can access our own inner wisdom and open to divine healing energy as well. Because we are not identified with them, we have a more fluid, expansive view of therapies and technologies. But when we dwell in the clutches of a naf, we are likely to resist even the most basic common sense. Nafs are extremely powerful in that they can keep us from accurately perceiving the unique conditions of the present moment.

Any and all available treatments—homeopathic, allopathic, naturopathic, meditative, pharmacological, surgical, dietary, clinically proven, and those whose effects are impossible to measure clinically—can be helpful when used in the appropriate situation. They are wondrous tools. Through intuitive wisdom, scientific experimentation, technological expertise, and divine love, they have been bestowed, discovered, or developed for the benefit of all.

Back to the Essential

The first day I was in medical school I learned a lesson from a plaque on a wall that read, "More than doctors, human beings." Whatever letters follow our name—M.D., M.A., B.F.A., C.F.A., R.N.—we will leave them behind after this lifetime. That includes our name itself. Yet I've come to discover there's something that doesn't stay behind, that always *is* us, and not just *with* us. What doesn't stay behind is our essential identity.

❖ **EXERCISE** ❖
WHO AM I?

This is an exercise we can use to begin to calm our minds, to bring them under our conscious control. Through this exercise we can begin to contact our soul. It can go on for a long time, and there are no "right" answers!

Relax your body. Now ask yourself, "Who am I?" Focus your consciousness on your head, and ask yourself, "Am I my thoughts?"

Now take your focus to each part of your body, resting briefly on your throat, your chest, your arms, your hands, your fingers, your solar plexus, your heart, your stomach, your pelvis, your legs, your feet, your toes. Ask yourself, "Am I my body?"

Now remember the last thing you ate and the last thing you drank. Remember the last music you listened to. Imagine the last flower you smelled. Remember the feel of your lover's body. Now ask yourself, "Am I my senses?"

Now bring your attention to whatever you are feeling at the moment. If you aren't feeling anything, imagine an extreme feeling that you have had recently. Perhaps you were really angry at someone. Now ask yourself, "Am I my emotions?"

Now focus on what you most love about yourself and what you most dislike. Perhaps you love it that you are really friendly to animals, and perhaps you hate it that whenever you get upset, you cry. Now ask yourself, "Am I my opinions about what is acceptable and what is not?"

Now focus on the people you love, those whom you are with every day. Now ask yourself, "Am I my relationships?"

Now turn your attention to your work, what you do every day, and ask yourself, "Am I what I do?"

Now focus on your religious beliefs, any identifications that you have in the spiritual realm, the church you attend, and ask yourself, "Am I my beliefs?"

Now imagine your face before you were born and ask yourself, "Where did I come from?"

Now imagine reading your obituary in the newspaper. What does it say? Are you your obituary? Ask yourself again, "Am I what the newspaper says?"

Now imagine yourself as a corpse. If you are lying down, you can rest yourself in this position. Imagine your body as old, grey, hard, dead. Ask yourself, "Where did I go?"

Now focus your attention on your heart and visualize it radiating golden light throughout your whole body. Ask yourself, "Who am I?"

PART TWO

---·❖·---

How We Heal

CHAPTER FIVE

---※---

God as Love, God as Gravity

The major illness of the twentieth century is not cancer or heart disease, but our lost connection to essence—our own and that of others and the world around us. I see health as wholeness rooted in realizing essential identity. Health is *not* the absence of illness; health is the awakened energy of essence. It is awake already, and we have the potential to awaken to it.

As a psychiatrist, I feel that at the root of every disorder lies false identification. Some psychiatric disorders are metabolic, some are genetic, some are enzymatic, some are socially induced. Of course, there are many effective therapeutic approaches to these disorders. But how an individual identifies himself is a vital part of the therapeutic equation. Our attachment to who we *think* we are keeps us from directly connecting with who we *really* are. This lack of connection leads to chronic stress, depression, and more serious mental and physical symptoms.

When we are attached to something and believe that we *are* that something, pain, suffering, disillusionment, and disenchantment inevitably appear. Those elements are synonymous with the realization of what truly is. The illusion of separateness and confinement they give us is exactly what enables us to expand our awareness and reconnect with essential identity.

It requires considerable courage, but if we open our hearts we can let pain, "bad" feelings, loss, and illness spur us along the evolutionary path to fourth- and fifth-dimensional awareness. The model of the healing pyramid presented in chapter 6 illustrates this process. Disease in particular can be a very wide gateway to realizing essential identity.

The pain that arises from an illness or the depression that arises from disenchantment—whether it threatens our life, our lifestyle, or both—may represent the first time that we encounter an obstacle over which we do not have even an appearance of control. It may be the first time we are challenged to slow down and appreciate the space between our heartbeats and the sacred quality of daily life. No matter what healing modality we choose— meditation, medication, dance therapy, or chemotherapy—surrender to essence becomes possible.

The strongest practice available to us as human beings is to consciously open to the force of infinite power and the force of the present moment. This practice aligns body, mind, and spirit in the unified field of divine love. It connects us to the higher powers of heaven and earth. This is surrendering to essence. This is where healing begins.

The Power of Surrender

If we can drop our attachment to ego, our attachment to temporary identities, and our attachment to health—even for a moment—the awakened world comes alive. Surrendering our attachments, like blowing the dust off a mirror, animates our true selves and the technicolor world of energy around us. The mystery of life cracks open and suddenly we are in it.

Through surrender, we give up human doing for human being. Aligning ourselves with the deep vibrations of positive feelings allows us to give up the busywork of our small minds. Through surrender, we abandon the confines of our ego-bubble. We stop clinging to false identifications; we let ourselves be. We let ourselves rest in the big picture.

What we are surrendering is who we think we are. What we are surrendering *to* is who we are. Actively surrendering enables us to enter into the natural flow of our essential identity. We accept. We become what we are, not what we are trying to be.

We can begin by surrendering to our immediate environment. By connecting with the higher powers of heaven and earth, we can consciously surrender our sense of fear and control. For example, recently I went sailing with a friend in Hawaii. The boat cut through the waves with the energy of a colt. The sails in the wind, the wind through my hair, the waves crashing against the hull of the boat—all hummed in a harmony that I felt vibrating through my veins.

Sensations like this can stretch our third-dimensional view beyond its ordinary limit. It's what a painter feels when the colors on a canvas begin to set up a magnetic tension and a living painting takes form. Or the feeling a father has when his infant smiles for the first time.

Every day we have thousands of occasions to stretch the limits of the small picture into the certainty of being. For example, one night around 11:00 P.M. I arrived at Chicago's O'Hare airport to teach a workshop on communication the next morning. I jumped into a cab and instructed the driver to take me to my hotel. A few minutes later I noticed that the driver was from India. I began to talk to him, telling him about my trips to his country. In the 1970s I had taught seminars there, and through them I got to know many members of Parliament.

The driver told me that he would like to introduce me to his grandfather, a master saint who had just arrived from the old country. It was late and I was tired. I was faced with choosing to proceed to my hotel or to open my heart to the presence of this cab driver.

Through the mirror, I looked into his eyes. Then I told him to take me to his grandfather. Some time later, forty-five minutes outside of Chicago, I found myself walking down the steps into a rundown basement. Inside was a beautiful man in his late seventies, wearing a turban. His aura was as bright as gold. In the heart-to-heart talk that followed, I found myself receiving meditations and prayers from him. We stayed up until sunrise. When his son later drove me to the hotel, I just had time for a quick shower and breakfast before giving my workshop.

That was the only time I ever saw that wonderful old man. Yet because I was willing to give up my own agenda, I was able to receive his teachings. After that, we corresponded for years and I received even more precious instructions that furthered my own well-being.

Another time, I was traveling in the South Pacific. My tour guide was a woman who, after taking me to one museum, asked me if I was interested in knowing a deeper aspect of her tradition. When I said yes, she said, "I'll pick you up at nine tonight."

It turned out that she was a granddaughter of the last

queen of Tahiti. When she arrived, she invited me to a ceremony that took place in the middle of the night. At the ritual that followed, I had the most formidable visions of human interconnectedness. I saw that each life form is connected to the others as in a web.

I could have been afraid to go out at night with a stranger. But in trusting my inner guidance, I made myself available for what I needed to learn at that particular time.

Every day presents a new opportunity to open our hearts, just as it lets us walk through the streets, go to the theater, work, study, grow. We can learn to actively choose to open to each moment of our lives without preconceptions, judgments, or expectations. We can appreciate what is around us, take what is offered, enjoy it, flow with it, even feel reverence for it. I call this "surrendering to the energy of earth."

Extraordinary situations also have tremendous power to wake us up to our essential identity. Often in the shock or afterglow of such events we are able to perceive the world as truly sacred. This is how an athlete feels after winning an Olympic medal, or a golf tournament. It's how a mother feels after giving birth. It's how an investment banker feels after striking a good deal. In these timeless moments we resonate with what truly *is*. We have the power to carry our victorious feeling forward into our lives. I call this "surrendering to the energy of heaven."

The power of surrendering to the ordinary and the power of surrendering to the extraordinary is the same: it puts us squarely in the present moment. Being in the present moment—no matter what gets us there—is a tool for remembering ourselves as essence.

The opportunities to surrender are as limitless as the breaths we take. If we commit ourselves to being in the present moment, our awareness will expand in a most organic way, like a tight bud relaxing into a beautiful flower. Although I cannot say that this path is effortless, I can assure you that it leads directly to an awakened sense of the abundance of our true selves and our surroundings.

THE FORCE OF HEAVEN, THE FORCE OF EARTH

Divine energy manifests in a tangible way as the natural forces of heaven and earth.

On the outer level, earth is the ground beneath our feet. We can take it in our hands, stamp on it. It changes with the seasons: wet, frozen, loose, friable. On the inner level earth is time, the material manifestation of the present moment.

The natural force of earth is *gravity*. If it weren't for gravity, the earth would have thrown us off long ago. Gravity keeps us grounded. Gravity is a gift. It means that while we're around, the earth loves us so dearly that it wants us close.

Heaven is the *space* around us. We can look up and see it whenever we like. Sometimes it is light, sometimes it is dark, sometimes it is obscured by clouds.

In the inner world, heaven is the realm of thoughts, ideas, feelings, and creativity.

The natural force of heaven is love. This divine love is part of everything. It is the web of interrelationship that makes the world around us. It is the love that brings a tree into being from soil, seed, sunlight, water, and time. Love is the cohesive energy of our experience.

The place where heaven and earth meet is the human

heart. When our awareness of these two forces is balanced, our hearts become the dancing ground of the divine energy of heaven and of earth.

"GOD IS GREATER"

Heaven and earth are bigger than human life, bigger than the bubble of our survival. But sometimes we are so self-absorbed that we forget to look up, or we have polluted the air so that looking up is impossible. Or we are obsessed with looking down, or with looking at ourselves—we lack the flexibility to look up. Yet it takes the sight of only one starry night for us to see that we're very privileged to be here, and we're also very tiny.

God manifests as gravity; God manifests as love. This reality is the paradox of heaven and earth. It involves knowing that we're subject to the force of gravity and also that we're bigger than our bodies. It involves feeling separate and yet being able to mix our energy with the energy of heavenly love simply by breathing. It involves knowing that we are going to die, and knowing also that we are eternal.

It's good to be small. In Jerusalem the phrase *Allah hu akbar* echoes from the towers and minarets. It means "God is greater." Whether you are the king, the beggar, the wealthiest merchant in the city, the wisest scientist at the university, the philosopher that knows everything, the most loving parent, the military officer who wins every battle—*Allah hu akbar*. God is greater.

In Jerusalem we also hear the chant *Shema Israel Adonai Eloheinu Adonai Ejat*—"Listen, O Israel, the Lord is eternal, he is one." Even the "I am" that comprehends the ego, the nafs, and everything in this creation is only a speck of light in the face of the divine. "God is greater; eternal; the sense of unity" is what surrender is all about.

Opening to the energy of earth, we open to gravity. Gravity is always here. Although we rarely relate to it consciously, it is hardly a neutral force. Like a lover, it draws us to the earth and holds us. We can relax in its arms. Opening to gravity involves resting in the delight of the physical world, including our own bodies.

Gravity is the passionate partner of our earthbound body. Through gravity we are anchored in a near-perfect world. We have a tangible, immediate, direct connection to earth.

The sun shines. Food grows. We breathe in oxygen; trees breathe it out. We have food to eat, water to drink, clothes to wear. We have variety: night, day, seasons. We have at least five senses, and the earth abounds in ways to delight them. Walking, breathing, sleeping, sitting, eating, drinking, we can let the earth support us. At this or any moment, we can surrender to the force of gravity.

Runners, skiers, Olympic athletes, even bungee jumpers play with gravity. Football players enjoy gravity. Carnival rides defy gravity. Astronauts go beyond gravity.

However, sometimes we forget the pleasures of gravity and resist being where we are. Then our disconnected ego, in defending its false identifications, in pledging allegiance to the small picture, expresses itself by erecting a fortress surrounded by a disharmonious symphony of thoughts that keeps us from hearing, seeing, touching, feeling what's really happening in the immediate physical world.

At such times we cling to our nafs, defending them with our very breath. Stress is the result. Our senses don't operate. Our muscles tense up. We breathe in a shallow manner, as if only our heads need air. Our reproductive organs stagnate. Our hearts palpitate. We are so controlled that we are hardly aware of our feet touching the ground.

Yet if we take the time to stop and feel our bodies on the earth, we find that the force of gravity is always there. We can surrender to it, like water flowing down a hill. We don't have to hold ourselves tight; the earth will do that for us. We can relax. When we relax, our senses open up. Our defenses fall down.

Instead of seeing what we think we see, smelling what we think we smell, hearing what we think we hear, feeling what we think we feel, tasting what we think we taste, we begin to see, smell, hear, feel, and taste the world as it really is.

This planet is a glorious place, empowered with the ability to engage our senses totally. When our senses open, the world becomes dynamic and alive. Perhaps for the first time since we were children we really see the blue sky, really smell the bread baking, really hear the call of loons, really feel clean sun-dried sheets against our skin, really taste a cherry.

As our senses open, the boundaries we had drawn around ourselves melt and the world becomes bigger. At the same time, we become bigger. Who knows where one ends and another begins? Our perception changes. We are able to operate on a deeper, more profound level. We are more efficient, more spiritually and physiologically available. We become part of the heavenly body of humanity. This is the world of embodied essence, the world of embodied soul.

THE DANCE OF CONNECTEDNESS

Once our awareness begins to expand, the world continues to open. As the world continues to open, so do we. We've found our partner and now we can dance.

The dance goes like this: we connect to our senses; we connect to the earth. We connect to the earth; we connect to our bodies. We connect to our bodies; we connect to heaven, the space beyond our bodies. Our bodies are awakened energy. The space beyond our bodies is awakened energy. We are empowered.

Living in our bodies—through movement, sports, or simply by resting and following our breath—is a way to live in the present moment, over and over and over again. When we genuinely relate to our bodily experience—even if we are merely sitting at a desk—it is impossible to be anywhere but on the spot.

Through beginning to disidentify with our nafs, we begin to experience a little space between our thoughts. With practice, we are able to recognize when we are caught in our story lines—"thinking" the world—and learn to reconnect with the present moment by shifting our awareness.

Being in the present moment breaks through our mental conditioning. We find that it's impossible to continue telling ourselves stories and at the same time be fully in our body in the present moment.

Temporary identities and the stress created by clinging to them are energy blockages. They block our access to essence. Being alert to the present moment is an extremely accessible gateway to essence. Once we know this, we always have a choice. We can be in the present or not. We begin to take responsibility for the state of our being. We see that rather than clinging to our nafs we can use them as a vehicle for remaining in the present.

In fact, we discover that we can use any ordinary activity as a means for stabilizing our expanded awareness: walking to work, washing the dishes, playing golf, writing a report, answering the telephone. If we commit ourselves to disidentifying with everything but essence—as the Sufis do—after a while we will no longer have a choice. Resting in anything but essence will seem unnatural.

MORE TOOLS FOR OPENING TO EARTH

There are more intense, disciplined, and formal practices we can follow in order to help ourselves open to the energy of the present moment. These include meditation, bodywork, and affirmations.

Meditation helps us learn to notice when we are thinking. We sit on a cushion and follow our breath; when our minds wander off, we bring ourselves back by labeling "thinking." In this way, we find out that we are not our thoughts. This gives us the power and space to stop acting them out. No longer are we slaves to a story line.

Bodywork can help us by decrystallizing emotional blockages that have manifested as tension in our bodies. Freeing blockages through Rolfing, acupuncture, massage, or other methods can in turn free us of old story lines that have solidified into physical baggage.

We can also use affirmations—positive speech—to make the stories that we tell ourselves more fluid. For example, a common reaction when something goes wrong is to say something like, "This just proves how stupid I am—I can never do anything right." If we have worked at creating some space for ourselves by letting the earth support us, we can now see our thoughts clearly enough to adjust that story to something like, "Well, I really blew it that time, but I'll figure out what happened, make some adjustments, and try again."

Chanting litanies called *zhikrs* is what Sufis do when they feel a nafs solidifying. Zhikrs are prayers that invoke one of the 99 attributes of God. If you are feeling low in self-esteem, for instance, you would repeat the zhikr *Ya Kabir,* which essentially means "The Most Great," 100 times each morning. As an antidote to feeling pressured by the lack of time, you could repeat 3,000 times *Ya Sabur,* or "The (Divine) Patient" in order to feel the quality of patience.

Evoking the attributes of God is helpful because in chanting them, we become neuropsychophysiologically immersed in the sound. Certain affirmations evoke energy frequencies that alter the biochemistry of the body, thereby restoring us to greater health. This is similar to mantra meditations in Hinduism.

When we're grounded in our bodies, we don't have to hold on to ourselves anymore. Gravity will do the work for us. We can throw all the energy we save by not holding on to ourselves into dwelling in the present moment. If we stay there long enough, we'll see that our body is not a closed system at all, but an open, vibrant, fluid, living teacher.

OPENING TO THE ENERGY OF HEAVEN

In opening to the energy of heaven, we open to space. Opening to space can be frightening. Space is groundless. There is nothing to lean on, no support. Space has nothing of the comforting, caressing quality of earth, which allows us to *be* and holds us with a passionate magnetic force.

Unlike the gentle opening of awareness that occurs when we open to gravity and let the earth support us, surrendering to the energy of heaven often comes through extraordinary events that shock us into waking up on the spot. These events can serve as a sudden initiation into who we are—essence. They include birth, death, illness, falling in love, disillusionment, and chronic pain.

When our daughter, Alexandra, was due to be born, I felt much joy at knowing she was coming. I was also in a great deal of pain, because my father had died forty days earlier. It was as if the angels that were bringing Alexandra to us were passing the angels that were carrying my father away.

Laura Huxley, Aldous Huxley's widow, had suggested to my wife, Carolina, and me that we explore Igor Charkovsky's waterbirth method. Alexandra had the first waterbirth in South America. Days before she was born, my wife and I spent our time meditating, holding each other and listening to music, creating a sacred space for the birth. When Carolina went into labor she wanted to be alone, so I left the house for a few hours to tell a close friend happy birthday. For a while I even got lost (in the city of my birth!)—apparently so that she could labor alone. When I returned we both got into a large tub filled with room-temperature water. First it was just Carolina and me, and then we were joined by a midwife. As the contractions came closer and closer together, I supported Carolina from behind. Finally the baby arrived.

I did the palpation, and mine was the first hand to touch my daughter's head. Her head came out, then her body came out, and then she stayed under water for some moments before we cut the umbilical cord. It was amazing to watch her stretch and seem to swim in this new aquatic environment, still connected to the placenta. It was 4:45 A.M. when we took her out and waited for the umbilical cord to stop pulsating. Then we cut the cord.

Then I prayed to bless Alexandra, and we jumped around in joy.

It just so happened that the two-hundredth anniversary of the French Revolution occurred two days after Alexandra's birth, and I was invited to a party at the French Embassy. There were over three hundred people there. The topic of the party, however, was not just the French Revolution. It was the talk about peaceful waterbirth. I started teaching classes on nonviolent birth at the medical school because of the press that Alexandra's birth received. What an initiation!

Birth is not that much different from death. When someone close to us dies, of course we will mourn. But we can acknowledge that we feel sad for ourselves, and send good feelings to the person who died. Again, we feel the sacred space of the present moment by surrendering to heaven and earth. Then we imagine ourselves taking in any emotional qualities that might be hindering the dead person's passage to the light: for example, fear, attachment, confusion, anger, and so on. We imagine their obstacles in the form of hot, thick blackness and breathe that in deeply. Then we send out to them anything we think they might need for their journey: light, love, courage, faith.

This is a way to connect with the divine intelligence that is flowing through our hearts, even in grief. Whenever we feel sad, we can breathe in our sadness and send out good wishes to our friend on the journey. This visualization, like all the others, can be as personal as we want.

Practiced with a text called Unlimited Friendliness, it is a practice performed at some Buddhist funerals.

These methods for working with negativity remind us that we are not alone. They harness our negative feelings into a positive power that undermines our attachment to our own small story and takes us into a bigger space. These methods might feel slightly insulting because we are embracing what we would normally avoid, but they allow us to surrender our resistance and accept the path of heart.

What we discover by doing exercises like these is that not only are we capable of transforming our negative emotions into unlimited friendliness toward others, but we are also capable of transforming them into unlimited friendliness toward ourselves.

If you believe that Jesus Christ died for your sins, you are acknowledging that he died for a much larger spectrum of pain than his own. It is an evolutionary perspective that offering up ourselves in suffering also might have the power to benefit others.

There are also ordinary ways to open to the energy of heaven. We start, as we do in connecting to the earth, by stopping. We take the time to stop and truly hear, feel, and see where we are. We become aware of the earth supporting us and relax into that support. Then we take a deep breath, not just with our chest but with our diaphragm, our abdomen. We take a good whole-body breath. We visualize ourselves breathing in through every pore of our bodies the divine love of the universe. Then we let go of that breath and dissolve into essence as it leaves our body. Now we are entering that sacred space. Then we take another breath.

There is more than enough divine love to go around, and it is always, always available.

Through focusing on our breath, we acknowledge God as divine love; we mix our smallness with the vastness of space. And as we mix our smallness with vastness, space—both inner and outer—opens up for us and we relax.

Like our bodies, our breath is a direct connection to the present moment. It is impossible to cling to ourselves when we're truly in the present moment. Through breathing, we connect to the heavenly space around us by exchanging ourselves with the universe. How many times do we breathe in a minute?

Connecting to the energy of heaven with our breath—in meditation or on the spot—also involves remembering inner stillness, inner space. Opening up to the divine love of the universe, we might for the first time since childhood become aware of a brilliant, silent space within.

This space is very vivid and real for children. For example, a friend tells me that as a child her recurrent sensation as she was falling asleep was of tumbling into an abyss of white light. As she grew older, the sensation of free-falling into this abyss became scary. She learned to "catch" herself—jolt herself awake just as she began to fall. As she became older still, she stopped falling and the mirrorlike white light disappeared. Now it is either perceived as a memory or a doorway of experience to access again.

Another friend remembers her older brother asking her, when she was about three years old, "Susan, please tell me what God looks like. I'm beginning to forget."

TOOLS FOR OPENING TO THE ENERGY OF HEAVEN

Tools like positive affirmations, other chanting exercises, and certain rituals use the element of simple repetition to connect us with a field that promotes a change in our metabolism, in our structure. We are repatterning or re-programming ourselves. It is as if we start to see with different eyes.

Ancient teachings ranging from Hasidism to shaman-ism have worked a similar neurophysiological transfor-mation through apprenticeship, or what psychologists refer to as modeling and what in Christianity is called mentoring. As an apprentice shaman, for example, one is taken through extraordinarily taxing rituals involving sleep deprivation, wilderness isolation, and sometimes sacred ritual plants in order to become a clear conduit for positive healing energy.

When we practice holding a positive model in our con-sciousness, we can connect with a higher knowing. For example, in Tibetan Buddhism practitioners go through the day visualizing their guru sitting on the crown of their heads. At the same time, they visualize all sentient beings as enlightened. My mentor in medical school, Dr. Ales-sandri, epitomized the caring, holistic healer I wanted to become. Sometimes I imagined a tiny representation of Dr. Alessandri in my head, there for me to call on for any courage or strength I needed in my practice.

Modeling a positive image brings about physiological and biological changes that will empower the newly learned pattern. It can also be used in business by visual-izing an imaginary board of directors comprised of the top business leaders of your field. Whenever you have the need of their expertise, you inwardly consult those individuals.

What Do We Get If We Surrender?

Surrendering to heaven and earth is a way to reactivate our direct line to the divine.

As St. Francis of Assisi said, "You can't stop the birds from flying back and forth over your head, but you can stop them from nesting in your hair." When we practice opening to the energy of heaven and earth, thoughts come and go like birds passing across the clear blue sky. We have a choice as to whether we focus on the birds or the pull of gravity at our feet or the infinite sky beyond.

The more space we feel, the more the living quality of the world is revealed. We no longer identify with our internal narratives, and a greater reality dawns. We begin to surrender control. We are no longer trying to hold our existence together with our heads and no longer trying to support our nafs with our bodies. As a result we have more energy and less stress. Discovering the power and gentleness of letting ourselves rest in the present, we begin to trust our own experience and feelings. Our hearts begin to open.

Using the force of the earth and the force of heaven, opening our hearts is what gives us the power to heal.

This shift of focus from the head to the heart can result in amazing instances of emotional and physical healing. Most of the time our life focus is cerebral: we are identified with what we think. Once our focus goes to the heart, we can reinforce our awareness of heart and of emotions, such as gratitude and love, that originate there. This spiritual path to the heart can also be a path to physical healing.

❖ EXERCISE ❖
CROSSING TO THE TIMELESS PLACE BETWEEN HEARTBEATS

At a time when you can be sure you will not be interrupted, lie down on the floor in a quiet place.

Now consciously begin to relax your body. Take a deep breath and say to yourself, "The earth will support me. I can relax."

Now, continuing to breathe deeply, consciously relax every part of your body. Start with the head. Think to yourself, "The earth is supporting my head. I can relax my head."

Move on to your torso. "The earth is supporting my torso. I can trust the earth to provide me ongoing support. I can relax."

Continue to relax every part of your body, including your organs, your muscles, your limbs, and your fingers and toes. Continue to breathe deeply.

When you feel deeply relaxed, begin to focus your attention on your heart.

Feel your heart beat. It is moving gallons of blood through your body. It will continue to do this, regardless of what you think. Relax your consciousness into your heart. Feel gratitude toward your heart for continuing to beat.

Now align your consciousness with your heartbeat. Imagine that it is a sacred drum, calling down divine energy with its beat. Relax into the beat.

Now, very gently, shift your focus to the space between your heartbeats. Let your mind rest there.

When you have stabilized the energy of your mind in the space between heartbeats, visualize that space as vast and filled with golden light. Rest your mind here. Imagine the space between your heartbeats filling your body with the golden light of essence.

Now imagine yourself dwelling in the space between heartbeats. Imagine that you are in a palace filled with golden light. Imagine that this is your home. There is infinite space here, and infinite love. The earth will support you in your true home.

CHAPTER SIX

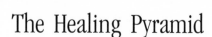

The Healing Pyramid

I have developed a model that I call the healing pyramid, which integrates every healing modality that the earth has to offer with the power of our open hearts and the power of heaven—divine love. As we ascend this imaginary pyramid, we are led to spiritual health and well-being. It condenses the process of surrender into a model of healing that incorporates the force of heaven at the apex, the force of earth at the base, and the path of the heart in the middle.

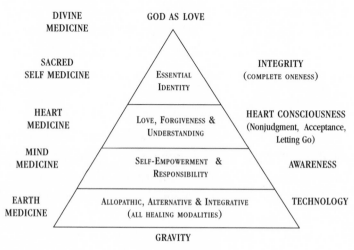

The illustration shows a view of the pyramid from its side—and at a distance. We see the energy of heaven streaming into the apex as love, while gravity grounds us securely on the earth.

As a structure the pyramid has broad contact with the earth, secured by the force of gravity. At the same time it aspires to the heavens, extending upward and outward, toward the vast spaces beyond. Each horizontal plane of the pyramid thoroughly permeates the level below it and above it. The apex of the pyramid is a point in space.

At each level of the pyramid from the bottom up, there is less ground and more space. This is an apt model for our own situation—held to the earth by gravity as the divine love of heaven fills the space around us.

The pyramid is also an apt model for the process of changing our residence from the confines of the small picture to the bright, infinite space of essence. Effecting this transition is at the root of every religious and spiritual tradition. Making the transition from confinement to freedom is also at the root of my vision of health and healing.

As you can see from the illustration, my model is divided into four parts. If you've ever climbed a pyramid, you know that it is easiest to see the part of the pyramid that is at your own level or below. The higher you go, the more of the pyramid you can see below you. As you look up toward the top, the rest of the pyramid looks very small.

The levels of the healing pyramid are like that. We can know the earth level very well and not ever be aware of the three above it, even though they are always available. However, as we expand our awareness to the other three levels, we find that our experience of the ground level becomes richer.

Earth Level

This is the level of every technique and healing methodology. This is the "well" we dip into when we need help.

At this level we are actively involved in doing things to improve our health. We consult practitioners in a wide variety of traditions, ranging from allopathic medicine to homeopathy to naturopathy to traditional Chinese medicine. All these traditions are equal in their effectiveness. This level also includes diet, exercise, botanical medicine, Ayurvedic medicine, and a myriad of other approaches to treatment.

At the ground level, the choice of the healing modality and the responsibility for healing reside with someone else—the family physician or another practitioner. We follow the advice of friends or family and practitioners: we deliver our bodies to someone to be fixed.

Tools for healing at this level include every methodology and type of healer available.

Heart Level I

At this next level of the pyramid, we are empowered.

Instead of heading directly to our usual doctors or healers, we survey all the healing traditions and choose the modalities that seem most appropriate for our condition. Of course we are wise enough to recognize that a chiropractor will not heal a skin rash, nor will an herbalist aid in aligning bones and joints. At this level we use our intuition, our own knowledge of ourselves, to choose a practitioner. We recognize that healing has to happen within and come from within. Whichever practitioner we choose can only facilitate that process. Even the most skilled healer cannot help us if we do not want to get well.

If our awareness opens to this level of self-responsibility, we will seek ways to fully engage our innate healing energy. We still have the same choices of healing modalities, but our approach to them is more interactive. We are empowered. We look for a healer who is also empowered—someone who treats people, not just symptoms. We trust ourselves enough to let our intuition guide our choice from a place of balance.

Trusting our intuition does not necessarily mean that at this level "intuitive" methods of healing take precedence over mechanistic approaches. It all depends on the situation.

When I was working in Argentina, I had a friend with an artificial heart valve. Since the valve replacement, he had started seeing a *curandero,* a type of faith healer and psychic surgeon. The curandero had helped this man through some emotional and physical problems, and my friend put a lot of faith and trust in his alternative healing methods. When he started becoming weak, it became obvious to me and to his physician that the artificial heart valve wasn't working well anymore. However, he refused to consider another surgery and a new valve.

The curandero promised that he could fix my friend's problems with psychic surgery, and I looked on as he spread an ointment on my friend's chest and seemed to plunge in his fingers and hand. The curandero was convinced that he had fixed the faulty valve, and my friend showed renewed energy—for a day or two. As he was about to return to the curandero for additional treatment, I convinced him to get a second opinion from a cardiologist, which he did. Finally he recognized that surgery was the best course of action. During the operation the cardiologist discovered that my friend had avoided certain death by a matter of days as a result of his choice.

At this level of the pyramid our toolkit includes everything on the first level, expanded by the addition of self-responsibility and empowerment.

Heart Level II

At this level we approach our condition with understanding, compassion, forgiveness, and love. We recognize that in some way we are responsible for our condition, although we may or may not have had control over the cause. For example, perhaps we were born with congenital anemia, or perhaps we suffer from emphysema caused by second-hand cigarette smoke. Regardless of the cause, at this level we learn to let go of any guilt, shame, or blame that we feel because we have these conditions. We learn to accept and tolerate the cause of the disease. This acceptance transforms any negativity we might feel into forgiveness and compassion. In the silence of the heart that follows, gentleness arises. We accept ourselves as we are and extend ourselves lovingkindness.

We have the power to heal ourselves. We choose to work with healers who are in touch with their own inherent healing energy and will help us arouse ours.

Tools for healing at this level include all those available

at the previous levels and also lovingkindness, compassion, acceptance, and forgiveness.

Heaven Level

Lovingkindness toward ourselves is the route to mastery in healing—the top of the pyramid. Here the self merges with the divine, where love of self becomes love of soul, all soul. When we reach the top level of the imaginary pyramid, when we have surrendered to self-love, we reach a frequency of coherence that is body, mind, and spirit—the frequency of essential identity.

Lovingkindness becomes a divine love, unconditional and all-embracing. It enters through our open hearts. We are able to radiate the luminous, healing power of this love to ourselves and others. We no longer fear suffering and are willing to "take on" the pain of others. We feel responsibility not only for ourselves but for a larger community.

His Holiness the Sixteenth Gyalwa Karmapa, spiritual head of one of the four lineages of Tibetan Buddhism, died of stomach cancer in 1982 in a hospital in Illinois. The doctors and nurses who cared for him were astonished and inspired by his kindness and cheerfulness in the face of excruciating pain. Toward the end of his life, when asked about dying, he said to one of his students, "Don't worry. Nothing happens." This exemplifies the view from the heaven level of the pyramid.

At this level we feel a certainty, a peace, a love that surpasses everything. Here it is obvious that we are on a journey—to the beloved, toward the divine. We are at one with ourselves, with others, with our surroundings—

indeed, with life itself—and that is the raw source of all healing. We wake up each morning grateful for life and the restoration of consciousness, and for everything else in the day. We wake up well.

Healing modalities at this level include all modalities available at the other levels, empowered not only with self-responsibility but also with divine love. In addition, we have community, selflessness, clear vision, and direct relationship.

❁ EXERCISE ❁
CLIMBING THE PYRAMID

In a quiet, relaxed place, lie down on the floor or the earth and imagine that an ancient pyramid incorporating all the wisdom of heaven and earth lies at the top of your head. At the base of this pyramid grow trees, roots, herbs, and flowers that contain all the healing energy in the universe. At the earth level of this pyramid, imagine all kinds of enlightened human beings whose mission is to help others discover their own essential wholesomeness and wellness.

Now you are going to climb the pyramid. First make your way through all the fauna and flora at the base. Imagine that you carefully step around each growing thing, taking care not to bruise its leaves or flowers. As you show your respect for these healing entities, they in turn shine forth, sending into your heart lightbeams of vivid color and healing energy.

Now you are at the first level of the pyramid. As you climb up the steps, the way is lined with healers of every race, religion, and persuasion, who are greeting you with warmth and light. There are doctors and nurses, homeopaths and acupuncturists, x-ray technicians and dentists, masseuses and dance therapists, priestesses and shamans. Every one has a unique, healing gift that is yours if you are open to it.

Now you are at the second level of the pyramid. Here you feel the heart-love of all those healers on the first level behind you as a force of light that propels you forward. You are awash in the goodness of human beings. This lights in you a wish that you may be well, and that others may be well. You realize that at any time you have the power to avail yourself of the strength and healing energy of the human spirit. You hold in your heart the wisdom to know what mode of healing energy would be best for you.

Now you are at the third level of the pyramid, and you feel your heart as a large, gleaming, translucent chunk of gold that contains everything you need to be healthy, wholesome, and helpful. This chunk of gold infuses you with light energy that transforms into vibrating gentleness and lovingkindness. At this level you imagine that you are absolutely perfect as a spiritual being, and at the same time you forgive yourself for seeing yourself as anything but divinely whole.

Now you are at the top level of the pyramid. Looking down, all you perceive is warmth, vibration, and golden light. Looking up, all you perceive is warm, joyously vibrating golden light. Looking to yourself, you find that there is no longer anyone there. Now imagine that the light of love at the bottom of the pyramid and the light of love at the top of the pyramid become one, and that the one is yourself. Feel yourself as fluid, golden light that is at one with the unified whole of the universe. Imagine that you contain all the healing modalities available to you, and that you are radiating them forth for others.

Feel the floor or earth beneath you. Condense the light of the pyramid visualization into your mind and heart, and imagine beaming it out as far as possible into the minds and hearts of others.

CHAPTER SEVEN

❖

Heart-Energy

The heart is the doorway to life. Every sacred tradition talks of a heart-based spirituality. In Christianity it is called the Sacred Heart of Jesus. Shamans talk about treading a path of heart. Followers of Sufism are often referred to as people of the heart. It can be understood emotionally, consciously, and spiritually, but it is important to realize that this doorway is also physical.

In the previous chapter we saw that at the second level of the healing pyramid we enter into the path of heart. At this level the path of heart involves cultivating inner awareness, empowerment, and responsibility.

About a century ago scientists discovered a node on the right auricle of the heart, which they called the sinus node. They noticed that the impulse that causes the heart to beat originates in the sinus node, not in the brain. Later, as science developed the technology to observe the development of the fetus in the womb, scientists discovered that the fetal heart starts pumping even before the brain is formed. Although it is obvious that things we ingest bodily or perceive mentally can alter our heartbeat somewhat, the important conclusion is that the heart has an autonomous nervous system with its own unique electrical field. It is here that the notion of "heart-intelligence" finds its grounding.

As we penetrate the vibration behind the heartbeat, the force that sustains the heartbeat, we can train ourselves to merge with the coherent frequency of love and of heart, which is the constant of life. As a flock of birds is so entrained that they all seem to take off, climb, and turn in simultaneous unity, so too can we feel ourselves perfectly in the flow of life when we remember to tread the path of heart.

I used a simple way to shift this awareness with a program called A Drop of Honey. Back in Chile in the late 1970s, when I first started teaching workshops, the country was hit by torrential rains and severe flooding. The first lady of Chile at that time, Mrs. Pinochet, went on television to appeal for donations to help the poor and homeless. Within hours, students from my workshops got together in a kindergarten building and filled it up with food, clothing, and supplies.

We went to the government that same afternoon and asked where we should deliver the donations for their relief efforts. They told us they didn't know; we had responded too quickly. The next morning, we ourselves were out in the poor and flooded neighborhoods distributing the supplies we had gathered.

At one point we came upon a line of homeless people. At the head of the line, representatives of a government social service agency were passing out donated clothing. As we talked to the social service people about how to coordinate our efforts, it was disturbing to hear them referring to those they helped as "dirty" and "lazy," calling them "stupid for placing their tents and lean-tos so close to the river." They disparaged us as well, scoffing at our idealism, claiming that what we were doing was like putting a tiny grain of sand on a vast beach.

However, we were having a much greater effect than they were. Like the social service workers, we were distributing supplies. The way we treated those in need, however, seemed to make all the difference. They seemed to appreciate the person-to-person contact as much or more than the supplies. I had been looking for an opportunity to have my students perform volunteer service as a graduation requirement for my program— some activity in which they could pass along what they had learned. That became the foundation of what was more than "A Drop of Honey"—a taste of a way of being that could motivate the needy to change their perspective permanently and therefore change their physical circumstances.

From that point on, Drop of Honey volunteers throughout South America (and later in such diverse locales as Washington, D.C., Kathmandu, and Los Angeles) would go into nursing homes, hospitals, orphanages, and prisons with the excuse of bringing gifts or supplies. Our real mission, however, was to gain entrance into these rigid bureaucracies to teach those inside about the path of heart.

For instance, we went to an orphanage in Venezuela. The staff told us that no one was allowed to visit the orphans. We told them we were there to distribute toys. At first they wanted us to leave the toys and let them distribute them, but we finally convinced the administrators to let us in to pass them out in person.

As we passed out the toys in rooms of a dozen or more cots, we asked the children to tell us their life stories. But we told them to listen to each other's stories in a different way than they were used to. We instructed them to imagine an ear on their heart or chest and to listen through that instead of through the ears on their heads.

Children of all ages noticed a change in how they related to each other with that simple shift in perception. The competition and restlessness about which the administrators had warned us disappeared. I remember one young girl in that orphanage coming up to me and saying thank you.

"You're welcome," I replied. "I hope you enjoy the doll."

"That doesn't matter," the girl told me. "I really liked the new way of listening."

Connecting with the Energy of Heart

Opening the heart allows for a connection with energies we may perceive as new, but in fact they have always been there. These energies are emanations of a universal intelligence. Hindus call this energy the Akashic record; Christians call it Sophia; Zen Buddhists, a minor encounter with *satori*. Kabbalists call it the Ayn Sof. The psychologist Carl Jung called it the collective unconscious, and indigenous peoples call it the group soul. More recently scientists such as Rupert Sheldrake have labeled it the morphogenetic field, or just the m-field.

It is a way in which any species, including humans, can access the knowledge and experiences of others of their species with whom they haven't ever been in contact. Scientists tie it to the way in which birds know to migrate at a specific time of year and to a specific location, without ever being taught. In humans, they theorize that it accounts for surprisingly rapid shifts in the aptitudes and abilities of humans all across the globe, beyond even what can be tied to the spread of information technology. For example, a man in Burma who has never seen a television, a telephone, or even a typewriter learns how to use a computer quickly because of all the experience with computers the rest of us have been adding to the field of universal intelligence over recent years.

The brain, the seeming depository of everything we can know, is better seen as a computer terminal, not as a mainframe. It can only function at the service of the natural universal intelligence when it is transduced through the *élan vital,* channeled via the heart. This is a nonlocal event, as physicists define the phenomenon. The heart is the mainframe.

Imagining the brain as the source of the natural universal intelligence we're talking about is like looking at a television or radio and assuming that each originates its own programming. However, we know that this is not the case. In fact, each electronic box is receiving a signal from radio and television stations far away over invisible airwaves.

We must recognize that those moments of breakthrough, intuition, or even memory are coming *through* that marvelous organ in our heads, but not *from* the brain. They are coming through the brain via the deep channel of the heart. As the Russian mystic G. I. Gurdjieff taught, access to the higher intelligence center is always through the opening of the heart center.

My work is the work of the heart. By "heart" I don't mean something gooey and emotional. What I'm talking about is a shift in focus, a path. Once this shift takes place and we start journeying through the doorway of the heart, spiritual work truly begins, because it's not separated from the outer; it's not separated from our ordinary lives.

The path of heart is a path of connection. The first step involves connecting with the present moment. Then we connect with ourselves by becoming aware of our inner world. We learn to shift our inner focus from the constricted path of the head to the wide-open path of the heart. Once we learn to do this in our inner world, we can use the path of heart to move forward through any situation that happens on the outer level.

Opening the Heart

Surrendering to the energy of heaven and earth, as we explored in chapter 5, is a way to practice connecting to the divine. By surrendering we are saying, "God is greater," and we thus acknowledge our existence in the larger context of the divine. We are releasing our hold on ourselves. We are acknowledging that we don't have to do it all, because it is all done.

After my father died I was praying in a temple in Santiago, Chile. I was wearing a yarmulka and it fell off. Then I felt his hand on my head. I had loved the feel of his hand on my head as a child and even as an adult. He had a big, powerful, strong hand. Whenever he put his hand on my head, I would feel relaxed and at ease and protected and taken care of. Now I had that feeling again. I turned around because I thought someone had walked by behind me and touched my head, but there was no one behind me and no one had walked by. It was physical. That is the sense of physical trust available to us when we surrender to the energy of heaven and earth.

Letting ourselves rest in the present moment gives us an opportunity to practice an interdimensional change of residence. We can shift our focus consciously from our head to our heart. By doing this, we are gradually expanding our awareness to include the living world of the invisible fourth dimension. This is more than a spiritual experience. It is what we need to do to develop a fifth-dimensional perspective, a unified field of vision which involves living from essence.

There is a place in each of us that is like a desert oasis reflecting the sun, or a beautiful garden of white flowers glowing in the moonlight. It is like a crystal-clear lake where not even the breeze ripples the waves, or a mirror on which there is not one speck of dust. This is the heart of hearts, and it lies at the inner core of our very being, between heartbeats.

This place is where we activate our realization of essence. It is also the place where we receive the divine energy of the universe. Through this place the natural intelligence of which I spoke earlier flows. Just as tuning in to the outer energy of the universe helps us access the present moment, accessing this place and learning to dwell there is the beginning of inner awareness.

It is from our heart that we begin to have the power to see who we are. The reason that cultivating the three qualities of lightheartedness is so important is that they allow us to see this place.

A while back I was flying from Seattle to Los Angeles to give a lecture. Because of a flight delay, I arrived at the Los Angeles airport only thirty minutes before the lecture was to begin in Santa Monica.

I was upset. I called my contact at the lecture hall and let her know what had happened. It was rush hour, and I was driving a rental car. I recognized that I had a choice. I could indulge in being upset—which did not change my basic situation—or I could "time out" my anxiety and focus on the presence of my heart. As I chose to do the latter, I was suddenly awash in gratitude for the company I had on the highway. Instead of complaining to myself about traffic, I felt completely grateful not to be alone.

At that moment, the car in front of me moved and suddenly I found myself passing cars right and left. In spite of the airplane delay and the traffic, I managed to reach the lecture hall only a few minutes late.

The power of experiencing the heart of hearts is that it gives us true freedom of choice. Of course, this freedom has always been there. First it was forgotten, obscured by temporary identities and our tightly woven cocoon of self-limiting thoughts, beliefs, and perceptions. Then the stress and inner conflict caused by clinging to this web closed us to it even further. But now, through learning to rest in the present moment without judging, through learning to accept, and letting go, we have the key to this quiet inner place. We see that it is quite possible to freely *be,* and that the choice is always ours to make.

Having even a glimpse of this space is like taking a baby-step to the greater reality of dwelling in essence. We can hardly expect ourselves to instantly strip off layers and layers of habitual patterns and jump into it. For most of us, remembering our heart of hearts only engenders the longing to live there always. This place is imminently accessible through certain techniques and practices—focusing on the breath and heartbeat, for example, or relaxing into a field of light that we visualize emanating from our chest. Remembering situations for which we are grateful also serves to open the heart. At the beginning we can hardly expect to dwell there throughout chaotic and stressful events that by their very nature trigger all our former defensive patterns. However, at this point what we can do is recognize our longing and aspiration to dwell in this place, and commit ourselves to it.

Our aspiration might take the form of finding a way to access this place in a protected atmosphere, where we are free of interruptions and outside demands. Try sitting quietly and relating to the most basic aspect of your physical being—your breath or your heartbeat, for example—so that you create a space in which you can see your thoughts arise. Then practice simply seeing them as thoughts. When your monkey-mind chimes in with a comment or judgment, you can label that "thinking" as well. If you do this for just a few minutes each day, you can train yourself in nonjudgmental observation by learning to recognize that you are thinking.

Continuing this practice on a regular basis will help you train in acceptance by resting with what is. Even if the thoughts keep coming—five, ten, fifty times—you can accept them for what they are by seeing them without judgment. Occasionally an especially enticing thought comes along and sucks us in for a while. Emotions in particular seem to have greater power than ordinary thoughts to draw us in. Sexual fantasies, anger at the boss, anxiety about the children—these are very powerful thoughts. But even if we jump into the river of our thoughtstream and swim there for quite a few minutes, the container of discipline allows us to see what we are doing and accept the thoughts for what they are. We don't try to push the thoughts away; our goal in moving from head to heart is not to stop thinking. We need to think. The point is to combine the wisdom of the heart with the clarity of the head. And we can't know clarity of the head until we've learned to master our inner world, moment by moment. The knowledge it takes to do that comes through the heart, not the head. Trying to clear our heads by stopping our thoughts would be like getting stuck in one of those Chinese finger-puzzles that are woven out of straw: the harder you pull, the tighter it gets.

I've used the example of meditation to demonstrate the efficacy of a formal technique, but there are many other ways to merge with the clear, quiet place we're talking about, where thoughts are obvious when they arise. These include among many others praying, gardening, flower arranging, and creative writing. When my wife, Carolina, was learning to sculpt, she experienced tremendous openness and flow, similar to what others describe in meditation. It is important for each of us to access our essence and our hearts by discovering our own way. The secret is passion.

Musicians, athletes, and dancers all know about this connection between the heart and the head. Ultimately, it is from their hearts that optimal performance—peak performance—flows. Any golfer knows, for example, that thoughts get in the way of a good putt. When a dancer dances, she is totally merged with the fluidity of the dance; any arising thought must simply pass through. When a pianist plays, he is completely at one with the music; if a thought arises, his playing is likely to falter.

The point is that there are many ways to train ourselves to dwell in inner stillness, and they don't all require physically keeping still. Wherever we feel a strong connection to the heart, that's the path to follow. The key to success lies in commitment and execution.

How Does It Work in Everyday Life?

When we practice opening the door to our hearts, we begin to contact our inner awareness. What does this have to do with healing?

By discovering this open, bright, quiet place within, we have begun to contact *ourselves*. We have entered the path of heart. We begin to take responsibility for our thoughts, our words, and our actions. When we can see the space behind ourselves, we can relate to that space instead of to our temporary identities and story lines.

When we're in the midst of a stressful everyday situation—even something as simple as working toward a deadline or waiting for a check that doesn't come—we can center ourselves in that quiet place instead of succumbing to our stressful, nagging story lines. This completely changes our relationship with stressful situations. It opens doorways. Meeting our heart of hearts is like opening a Russian nesting doll, except that instead of getting smaller and smaller, the worlds we open to get bigger and bigger. To stretch the metaphor to its outer limits, I'll tell you that it's not the *worlds* that get bigger and bigger, it's our hearts that expand.

To illustrate what entering the path of heart is all about and why it's such a healing path, I'm going to contrast what happens in a "blind" reaction to stress with what happens when we're coming from the empowered, responsible path of heart.

STRESS AND THE PATH OF THE HEAD = BLIND REACTION

When we're in a stressful situation and we have no inner awareness, our first reaction is often a knee-jerk response based on past conditioning. This is related to following the path of the head. Here to illustrate this phenomenon is a morning in the life of Dan.

Dan wakes up late. His wife berates him for not noticing that they're out of breakfast tea. His daughter can't find her favorite T-shirt and won't get dressed until Dan finds it for her. Dan feels angry. He shouts at his wife that she also could have noticed they were out of tea, and he shouts at his daughter that she can very well find her own T-shirt in that disaster area she calls her room. Dan's wife shouts back; there's plenty of colorful language on both sides. She stomps into the bathroom and slams the door. Dan's daughter bursts into tears.

Dan is furious. Adrenaline is flooding his body, his heart is beating rapidly, and his breathing is shallow. He's experiencing stress. His physical symptoms reflect the authenticated biological "fight-or-flight" response to danger, our automatic response to stressful events.

Acting out negative emotions by having a fit can be seen as both fight *and* flight: we're creating discord and at the same time we're flying off the handle into a hyper-emotional realm. We're resisting our own irritation or frustration by inflating it into aggression and aiming it at an outer object of blame.

The physiological reactions are in themselves stressful. In stressful situations that threaten our survival they give an extra boost in our fight or in our flight, but in a stressful situation that threatens our ego-bubble they simply flood our bodies with toxic stressors.

Our response to this continued buildup of stress is to seek resolution. Dan now apologizes to his wife, for example, but his wife is acting out her anger, too, and won't accept his apology. This makes Dan furious, but he doesn't say anything else as he storms out of the house. Now Dan is repressing his negative emotion. This process is really not all that different from acting out, although it may prove less harmful to others. He's still resisting his original feeling, but now by inflating it into anger and aiming it at an *inner* object of blame—himself.

Dan is experiencing the stress of the original situation. On top of that is the stress created by his dysfunctional response to the original situation, and on top of that is the stress created by his trying to resolve the stressful situation created by his dysfunctional response. On top of it all, Dan is now late for work. He feels more stress. He rushes out to his car, turns on the ignition, and guns it out of the driveway, narrowly missing another car. This is another knee-jerk response, this time bordering on self-destructive behavior.

Dan works in marketing, and he's got a big presentation to make. He can't blow it by being late. He's saying to himself, "I *can't* be late, I *can't* be late, I *can't* be late." But guess what? He *can* be late. Every red light becomes another stressor. To calm himself down, he lights up a cigarette. But smoking merely reinforces his physiological symptoms. By the time he arrives at work, he's again in complete stress mode: adrenaline pumping, heart beating rapidly, breath shallow.

Anxious because he's late, Dan barges into the conference room. His colleagues have been waiting for him, and they're feeling a little impatient. They find his long, "poor-me" explanation of why he's late boring. He's not the only one whose day ever got off to a bad start. His presentation goes fairly well, although he's still so angry at his family and so conflicted about having been late that he isn't really present for it.

The boss asks Dan some questions at the end, and Dan feels attacked. To defend himself, he tells the boss about a similar situation he faced in his last job. The solution he's presenting now worked in that instance, so why not in this one? The boss looks as if he'd like to ask more questions, but Dan's speedy delivery and airtight logic have effectively ended their interchange.

Back in the privacy of his own office, however, Dan begins to worry that maybe the presentation didn't go quite as well as he thought. He feels he might have missed something. He telephones a good friend for solace but instead finds himself complaining bitterly about his family, his job, and his boss. He asks his friend to go with him for a drink at lunch, but his invitation is met with a lame excuse. His friend has had enough of Dan for one day. Dan feels anxious, helpless, defeated, rejected, and at the mercy of what might happen to him next.

This is an example of a stressful day, which most of us have had on more than one occasion. Notice that Dan's experience is characterized by passivity. He's outer-identified and easily overtaken by stressful events. His reactions to what happens are closed and defensive. He has no choices. Poor Dan, today he is securely locked into the path of the head.

The Circular Quality of Stress

Stress leads to more stress, and then to superstress. Our bodies become accustomed to this hyper-aroused state. We learn to maintain it through addiction and other self-destructive, self-defeating coping mechanisms. In and of itself, stress can become addictive. Our immune systems become chronically compromised. This leads to stress-related disease.

There are a number of stress-related diseases that are related to "fight"—high blood pressure, heart problems, depression, cancer. Other stress-related diseases seem more related to "flight"—addiction and other self-destructive coping behaviors. The "fight"-related diseases tend to develop slowly over time, often exacerbated by the "flight" responses, which are often entrenched in habitual patterns dating from childhood.

Wherever our stress takes us, when we respond to it with knee-jerk reactions we are left feeling frustrated, powerless, and at the mercy of outer conditions. We may even become so stressed out that we keep ourselves in a mild state of "fight or flight" at all times. We make stress into a temporary identity called crisis mentality. Needless to say, this has a negative impact on our physical well-being.

STRESS AND THE PATH OF HEART = CHOICE AND POSITIVE INFLUENCE

Now I'm going to draw a picture of the same day from the perspective of someone who's accessed the silent voice that dwells between heartbeats. Now we're on the path of heart, which bestows responsibility and empowerment.

Bonnie wakes up late. She feels pressured to get to work early, there's a run in her stocking, and the dog pees on the floor. Her husband, who is also in a hurry, is upset that she hasn't made his lunch. Her son comes into the kitchen whining that he can't find his favorite T-shirt. Something pops in Bonnie and suddenly she's furious. She'd like to throttle her whole family, and that includes the dog.

Adrenaline floods in, Bonnie's heart starts beating rapidly, and her breathing is shallow. She sees what's happening: she's angry. Her first impulse is to engage in a shouting match; she just doesn't know whom to shout at first. But she's able to catch herself. Instead of yelling, she takes a very deep breath.

Even though Bonnie hasn't acted out her anger, her family understands that she's really mad. They see that she obviously feels angry and yet she hasn't flipped out. In fact, they're so amazed by Bonnie's behavior that they take a deep breath, too. Now the atmosphere is calm—completely different than it was only a minute ago.

With a little self-awareness and one deep breath, Bonnie has short-circuited her fight-or-flight response. She's come back to earth and opened up the inner space of her heart. Not only that, she's avoided having an altercation with her husband and son. But she hasn't avoided her *feeling*. She knows she feels furious. However, since she's not in the height of a knee-jerk reaction, she can anchor herself firmly in the present and find resolution.

Now she's able to open up the space around her, too. She calmly tells her husband that if he can't make his own lunch, he'll have to eat out. She informs her son that if he can't find his T-shirt, he'll have to wear something else.

Bonnie's running a little behind schedule, though, and she's going to be late for work. Driving to work, she seems to hit every red light and traffic is heavy. At each red light, she feels frustrated. She wishes she had a cigarette, but seeing as how she stopped smoking months ago, she's glad she doesn't. Instead, she takes the opportunity to ground herself by breathing deeply as she's waiting for the light to change.

Bonnie knows she's going to be late for her big presentation. She knows she's doing the best she can and drops her anxiety by engaging herself totally in her driving. Now she finds herself actually enjoying the challenges of navigating the heavy traffic. Again, stress has been headed off by a positive response.

Right before walking into the meeting room, Bonnie feels overwhelmed by anxiety. She takes a moment to close her eyes and visualizes a bright light radiating from her heart. Then she takes another deep breath, smiles, and walks into the room. Her colleagues are impatient that she's late. She apologizes and shares with them a brief, lighthearted account of her morning. Everyone laughs. They've all had days that start this way, and the fact that Bonnie can see the humor in hers lightens the whole situation.

The presentation goes well. The boss asks some questions at the end, and Bonnie feels defensive. She sees that she's about to panic. Instead, she focuses on really *listening* to what her boss is saying. She uses her senses to return to the present moment. Ah-hah! Now she sees that he's not *attacking* what she presented—he's just curious about it. Her answers lead to some lively banter. Everyone participates, and a creative brainstorming session is the result.

After the meeting Bonnie feels energized. Retreating to her office, she telephones a good friend to see if she'd like to go for a walk at lunchtime.

This is an example of a morning that could have been stressful, but wasn't. In facing potentially stressful events, Bonnie acted with awareness and openness, which led to flexibility and spontaneity. The key to her experience is that at each stressful point Bonnie *made contact* with the present moment, acknowledged her feeling, opened her heart, and took responsibility for her action. She could do this because she is inner-identified with the quiet voice of the heart.

WHAT'S THE DIFFERENCE?

The difference between Dan's morning and Bonnie's morning is that Bonnie was able to step back and see what was happening at any moment from the perspective of awareness. Dan's reaction reflected the attitude, "Why is this happening to *me*?" and had the effect of limiting his choices in terms of how to respond. He ended up being boxed in by stress and feeling victimized and powerless in the face of outer events.

On the other hand, Bonnie's response reflected the attitude, "What can I learn from this situation?" and opened doors for her. Every time a new door opened, she felt more empowered.

To each new stressor, Bonnie responded from the path of heart. As a new stressful situation appeared on her horizon, she noticed what she was feeling, accepted it, and let it go. Then she threw herself fully into what was happening. By participating with the external event, she was able to create a positive outcome in every case. This increased her feeling of empowerment.

Dan, on the other hand, was not in contact with that larger point of view. As a result, he wasn't really in contact with himself either. His reactions to what happened to him seemed based in the past. He withdrew from the stressful situations. Rather than participating, he tried to escape—through acting out his negativity, through retreating into addictive patterns, through defending his "territory," through solidifying a "victim" identity. All these repetitive, knee-jerk reactions repeatedly failed to get him what he wanted. Instead of making his world bigger, they made it smaller. As a result, he felt helpless and powerless.

This is a vicious circle. When we feel helpless, we tend to back away from any kind of stressful situation. Yet stressful situations are impossible to avoid. Taking a basic stance of helplessness only heightens how threatened we feel by them. Studies show that people with this stance are the most likely to fall ill when stressful events arise, because they have not developed the inner resources to respond in a positive way. Their attitude of helplessness can be more damaging to their immune systems than even the stress itself.

On the other hand, people who have developed attitudes of hope and curiosity and involvement in whatever is happening around them are able to live longer, healthier lives. They believe that they do have the ability to positively influence events, and they are willing to *act* on that belief rather than be victimized by circumstances. They feel stimulated and challenged by change. When we feel like this, we can react as Bonnie did to stressful events by *increasing* our interaction with them. We dive into them, explore them, learn from them, and even welcome them.

Taking the path of heart also has a circular quality. Every time we do it, we are strengthening our sense of responsibility, empowerment, and awareness. Not only do these attitudes arise from opening our hearts, they also open our hearts further. Hope, connection, creativity, empowerment, and responsibility are healing attitudes. They buffer the harmful effects of stress. They have a forward-moving energy that keeps us sailing through any situation we encounter. When we align ourselves with them, our world becomes a bigger place where we have infinite choices and the power to create positive situations for ourselves and others.

Staying on the Path of Heart

In dealing with stress, five basic steps can keep us on the path of heart. As soon as we become aware of a stressful situation, we can:

1. *Tune in to the breath.* As we have seen, taking several breaths deep into the belly anchors us. Through taking a deep breath, we surrender to the energy of heaven—clear space. This opens the door to the heart, supplying the stability we need to see our habitual reaction.

2. *Return to the present moment.* By feeling our physical heart, we surrender to gravity and return to the present moment. Remaining centered in the present moment allows us to see clearly what is going on, both in the outer situation and in our internal response to it.

3. *Expand inner awareness.* Our hearts are open, and we are firmly in the present moment. Now we can observe whatever arises in us—anger, fear, pain, tension, a pounding heart, sweaty palms, churning stomach, a desire to run or to protect ourselves. We are fully aware of what is happening without being caught up in it. We accept it and let it go. We actually shift our focus to the heart, eliciting gratitude and love.

4. *See the "big picture."* Remaining aware of the entire context of the inner and outer situation, we are able either to *maintain* inner calm and balance or to *recover* it quickly if we have temporarily "lost it."

5. *Exercise new options.* In the clear space of inner equanimity, creative approaches to resolving the stressful situation now arise. Our new options are

infinite, but we can begin with an affirmation, a prayer, an offering, or simply by tuning in to higher emotional frequencies (which we will discuss in chapter 8).

Choosing the path of heart does not mean that we will never feel threatened or fearful or angry. It does mean that we will be more aware of these feelings when they arise. We are not trying to suppress our emotions when we respond to stress; rather, we are cultivating a deeper, broader awareness so that we can see both our inner and outer situation more clearly and respond more effectively and appropriately. Deeper awareness leads to greater understanding, which leads to more choices in dealing with stressful situations.

When we bring inner awareness to stressful situations, we can take responsibility for any emotions that arise. For example, we may be aware at times that we are overreacting, that our emotions are out of proportion with what is actually happening and are based on an old core belief. Keeping the broad perspective of essence at these times, however, will allow us to discharge the emotion and bring our response back into balance. We will see this event as an opportunity to dispel yet another illusion.

Choosing the path of heart and maintaining connection with essence when under pressure is empowering. As relaxation and inner awareness become a way of life, it becomes easier to call on them when we need them. They replace our former automatic stress reactions.

Everyday Ashrams and Monasteries

In describing how the path of the heart begins, I have
purposely used an everyday situation, because our everyday lives are where healing starts. Our households and
our workplaces are ashrams for practicing the healing
path of the heart.

If we use ordinary events as opportunities for waking
up to essence, then when extraordinary situations (such
as illness) arise, we have a well of inner resources from
which to draw. We know how to use external events to
open worlds of choices for ourselves and others.

Opening our hearts not only puts us in touch with the
inner wisdom that is at our core, it also opens the way to
clear seeing so that we are able to engage our minds in a
much larger vision than we ever dreamed existed. Following the path of heart takes us into a phenomenally
wealthy world where contact, communication, relationship, and service to others are always available.

God's will is found in the chambers of the heart. If we
try to understand moving toward the light of essence from
a head perspective, we will be frustrated because we'll
encounter all the limitations of the path of head: beliefs,
preconceptions, mindsets. If we remain in the heart perspective—observing without judgment, accepting what
happens, and letting go—we can see our journey through
life as an interdimensional ride. The more we live from our
hearts, the more understanding we'll have.

Treading the path of heart has nothing to do with religious beliefs. It goes beyond belief and concept into
resonance and positive action. For example, I was recently in southern Tennessee, where I was interviewed
on a television program by a black Baptist host. At the
end of the program we looked into each other's eyes, and

we loved each other. He said, "But we don't *believe* in the same thing." I said, "Look, husbands and wives don't believe in the same thing—why should you and I believe in the same thing when we just met? But there's one thing we can do: we can connect in the resonant field of the heart. We can learn and love each other from there!" And he answered, "You are right on!"

❖ EXERCISE ❖
OPENING THE HEART

Opening the heart is easy. Opening it is like opening an eye. It isn't like saying, "Oh, everything's so nice, everything's so beautiful." It involves rotating a wheel that is a portal for our attention to go through. The opening of the heart is an act of surrender and will. Will is located below the heart in the solar plexus. To relax the solar plexus, take a few deep breaths. Breathe deep into your belly. Relax it.

Relax your solar plexus and stay relaxed. Then relax your belly. Concentrate the will that's there to say, "I am going to open my heart, *now.*" It doesn't happen from the outside; it happens because you allow it, you will it, you determine it, you commit to it.

How does it feel? How can you find a road inside the heart that leads to the divine intelligence? Stay in your heart. Listen to each beat. Soon you will feel a tunnel that goes to someplace else. This tunnel gets opened with practice. Try doing this practice every day for a week.

As you go about your business after practicing opening your heart, continue to reconnect with what you feel in your solar plexus. Even in stressful situations—especially in stressful situations—focus on the heart. Open it up. What do you feel there?

CHAPTER EIGHT

---※---

Inner Work

Words, sentences, paragraphs, and chapters like these follow each other in a linear manner. The path of heart, however, although evolutionary and forward-moving, is not linear. The personal journey to the core of one's very being, acknowledged universally by every wisdom tradition, is uniquely serpentine in nature. It is a spiral, a circle, a holographic mandala, through which larger and larger dimensions open. If we were to draw a picture of this journey, it might resemble the double helix of DNA, or the snakes encircling the caduceus (the ancient symbol that even in drugstore logos we still recognize as the emblem of healing).

In this chapter we tread further on the path of heart. This reflects the third level of the healing pyramid, in which we open our hearts to the cultivation of positive emotions such as forgiveness, love, compassion, and understanding.

Opening the heart further is a powerful tool for interpersonal and social transformation. It leads to the essence of true self-esteem. It reduces personal, family, and job stress. It is the key to inner awareness and fulfillment. It is the only route to realizing our essential health and well-being.

How the Heart and the Brain Work Together

The heart is a life-sustaining, blood-pumping organ. It has an electrical energy field that translates into a frequency forty times wider than the electrical field of our brains. Electrically, its power stirs deep feelings of hope, love, and care. It is also the "ear" for listening to the source of higher intelligence.

Tuning in to these positive feelings and the higher intelligence enables us to make positive choices. Accessing it through our inner voice gives a sense of inner knowing. Experiencing love, care, and compassion produces a qualitative shift in the electromagnetic field of heart: it makes it larger.

The brain is our center of intelligence. It thinks, analyzes, and processes information and data. It reads out data from the five senses; from the heart; from the paracrine, endocrine, and immunological systems. It is truly our CPU (central processing unit).

When the heart inputs its intuitive intelligence, the brain translates the frequencies into thoughts, symbols, words, and concepts so we can understand and act on them. By following the directives of our hearts instead of staying tuned in to habitual mental images, we allow our brains to perceive congruently with our open hearts. Coherent, congruent, and confluent actions follow. The union of body, speech, and mind that results is true well-being, because it is in alignment with our essential identity.

Holographic Awareness

Our awareness travels in more than one way. It is outside-in, and inside-out. It permeates in all directions: east, west, north, south, and also up and down. It is fluid, vibrating, and vital. It changes all the time. It is holographic.

The world we perceive through the senses is an ocean of frequencies that the brain translates into the third-dimensional world, a holographic image that we call reality. As recent findings in quantum physics confirm, we are co-creating reality, not just discovering it.

In *Wholeness and the Implicate Order,* physicist David Bohm says:

Relativity and quantum theory agree in that both imply the need to look upon the world as an undivided whole in which all parts of the universe, including the observer and his instruments, merge and unite in one totality. A new form of insight implies that flow is in some sense prior to that of the "things" that can be seen to form and dissolve in this flow. That is, there is a universal flux that cannot be defined explicitly but which can be known only implicitly, as indicated by the explicitly definable forms and shapes, some stable and some unstable, that can be abstracted from the universal flux. In this flow, mind and matter are not separate substances. Rather they are different aspects of one whole and unbroken movement.

In the previous chapter, we saw how Bonnie created one reality by consciously activating frequencies of her heart that allowed her to think and act so that her influence was positive and her experience was progressive. She kept moving forward into open space. Dan created a completely different kind of reality by aligning himself with old mental images that effectively kept him running into brick walls.

Through both examples, we saw how everything is interconnected—our emotions, the way we drive a car, how we relate to others, how they relate to us. We are part of this open system, and as such we always have the power to actively choose a different holographic picture by accessing the higher frequencies of the heart. Through devotion to the path of heart, we can change the future at any moment. The choice is ours.

If we consider the *terminal*—the brain—to be the seat of consciousness, we tend to flatten our holographic awareness into a small screen in our heads. Then we project this imaginary screen out onto the world around us, in effect flattening our perception.

But if we acknowledge the seat of consciousness to be the heart, our experience is totally different. We see that in truth, we are a door. Through the awareness of the heart, our consciousness is an open door, a portal, not just something that receives images through our brains or projects images on the small screen of the "objective" reality of the third dimension.

Ironically, regarding the brain as the seat of consciousness only leads to clouding the clear, diamondlike quality that the brain has when receiving the *heart's* intelligence. The brain is the transducer for the heart's wisdom. Unclouded by our core beliefs, the brain works in tandem with the heart, guiding us directly and straightforwardly on our path as a soul who is having a human experience. Allowing the brain to do its job efficiently is a matter of *unlearning* the core beliefs of the head, while at the same time tuning in to the energy of the heart.

When we are identified with the path of the heart, the

brain enables us to see ourselves and others clearly, to speak with meaning, and to act from the higher frequencies of the heart, which we call *core values*.

By awakening the energy of our hearts, we give ourselves the power to release judgments, communicate honestly, enjoy inner self-esteem and security, and uncover the frequency of compassion. We can surrender to the higher intelligence and power that enters through our hearts.

The coherent frequencies of the heart also have healing power. By tuning in to the higher frequencies (shifting from anger to forgiveness, for example) we can lower our blood pressure and increase T-cell counts. As stress subsides, these systemic and immunological changes take place. Thus, tuning in to the holographic awareness of the heart can be a way to change the frequency patterns that cause illness. From there, the activation of the heart takes place and we can forgive ourselves and forgive others, magnetize our appreciation and caring, and see even death and dying as a frontier on which to move toward the light.

Love is the core energy of the heart. It is also the energy of expansion, of connection. It is the vital, divine current of creation. When we tune in to this higher-dimensional energy, we return to core human values.

Core Values

Core values such as forgiveness, understanding, compassion, and lovingkindness are essential human values. They don't come from the brain; they come from the heart. These values embody the natural energy of the human heart.

Heart values are fluid. Through the open doorway of the heart, they flow *out* and they also flow *in*. They make a bridge between what we so often see as our "separate self" and the vast ocean of the interdimensional, interconnected world around us. They are the vehicles by which we express the essential fluidity of our being; they are the means by which we receive the divine energy we embody. These values connect us with others. Opening to these core values, we no longer feel or see ourselves as separate. At the same time, we can see others as ourselves.

When we identify with lower frequencies such as anger, fear, depression, apathy, boredom, anxiety, irritation, frustration, exhaustion, low self-esteem, unfulfillment, tension, discouragement, and stress reactions, we are damming (and "damning") these higher human values. Solidifying the lower frequencies blocks the love, forgiveness, and compassion that dwell in our hearts. It keeps us from entering the human realm, which is also the realm of the divine.

In blocking the love, compassion, and forgiveness of our hearts, solidified negative emotions lock into our bodies an explosive force that, if unchecked, will create disease. They are like sticks of dynamite that sooner or later will implode into heart disease, kidney failure, cancer, severe depression, or a fatal accident. Unfortunately, because we hold on to negative emotions, some of us die with a lifetime of love still locked up in our hearts.

One interesting phenomenon, readily experienced on the path of heart, is that it takes much more energy to harbor negative emotions than it does to let them go. Granted that it's important to acknowledge them. It's also important to *feel* them. And we're going to explore fluid ways to work with them. But after doing that, it takes much more energy to retain the negative feelings—clinging, grasping, defending, clutching at, holding a grudge—than it does to flow with the gentle path of heart. Touching our hearts, feeling our hearts, takes us beyond these negative emotions into higher frequencies, such as forgiveness. We don't have to *create* these higher frequencies; they are already there.

Inner work entails *unlearning* our attachments to the lower frequencies. We will always experience the lower frequencies, but we can learn to work with them in creative ways. We could consider inner work as simply "attention to essence." The more we attend to essence, the less likely we are to let temporary identifications crystallize. Inner work unblocks the dam and allows our true heart power to flow naturally. As well, it clears our hearts so they can actively receive the divine energy that flows around us and through us.

The different wisdom traditions and religions have reinforced those core values through their moral codes and prayers, rituals and practices. The Bible tells us, "Love thy neighbor as thyself." Tibetan Buddhists say, "Be grateful to everyone." The Sufi sage Hadrat 'Ali said, "Faith is experience by the heart, avowal by the tongue, and action by the limbs." These traditions know that higher heart frequencies are the doorway to cosmic intelligence. Cosmic intelligence is running the show.

Frequencies of the Heart

Some of us repress our emotions, some of us act them out. Some of us try to suppress others' emotions. None of these approaches works. On the path of the heart, we learn to see our emotions clearly and manage them. And in managing them we find out that any emotion presents an opportunity to connect with essence.

We quickly learn that when we align our emotions with the wisdom of the heart, we have fun. The more we listen to the heart, the more we hear it. I find it useful to think of emotions as frequencies we can tune in to.

We can visualize higher and lower heart frequencies, higher and lower bands of emotions. It's as if the universe were filled with radio stations or television channels with their own patterns—their own sonics, their own design and texture. Each station is tuned to a band or to many bands at different times. These are the dimensions. Although some frequencies affect us subconsciously and we can't do much about them, we have a choice of how to respond when we're aware of them.

For example, the thought "I forgive myself" is powerful because it cuts through our story lines. It cuts through them because it resonates with a higher frequency of emotion than the thought "I am bad because I have made myself sick by eating the wrong foods." Saying with commitment and devotion "I forgive myself" transcends the static electricity of the lower frequencies of emotion. It doesn't try to obliterate them; it doesn't argue with them. It rises above them.

If we tell ourselves with conviction "I forgive myself" and feel it in our heart of hearts, then the other story lines—"I'm a lousy person because I did this-and-this-and-this," "I can never do anything right," and so on—simply wither and die in the face of the truth.

The energy of "I forgive myself" is the affirmation of the truth. It engages a transformative energy—the energy of forgiveness.

When I arrived in Colombia from Venezuela, it was

during fierce contention between the two countries for fishing rights. In Cartagena, I gave a workshop for some business leaders. In one of the exercises I asked the participants to accept and love themselves. I then directed them to accept and love their colleagues. After they had done this, I asked them to extend these high-frequency feelings to customers and even competitors.

Then I asked the participants to accept and love all their fellow Colombians, especially at this particular time of strong nationalist feelings. Few of them had trouble accepting and loving all the other citizens of their own country. Finally, I asked them to accept and then love the citizens of Venezuela. To my surprise, most of them were in such a loving space after the first part of this exercise that they were able to do this—all except one woman. She told me angrily that she had no intention of accepting or loving Venezuela or Venezuelans. In fact, she hated Venezuelans.

I asked, "Have you ever been to Venezuela?"

"No," she answered.

"Well then," I prodded, "do you know any Venezuelans?" Again she answered no.

"Where did you feel the love for your competitors?" I inquired.

"Inside myself," she answered.

"And where do you think your hatred for Venezuelans exists?" I continued.

"Since I don't know any Venezuelans, I think that I am really hating that part of myself that doesn't accept them," she replied.

On hearing that insight, a Catholic nun among the participants cried out, "Merciful God!"

"What is it?" I asked the elderly nun.

"I have served the Church for over fifty years," she said with tears running down her cheeks, "and this is the first time I really knew what Jesus Christ meant when he said to love one's enemies as oneself!"

In Hinduism *sanskaras* ("impressions on the soul"), or what we are calling crystallized false identities, are erased or healed through attunement with the frequency of forgiveness. Hindus believe that sanskaras impact the life force of the heart; they represent a cycle that we are forced to repeat until they have been removed from their hardened position on our hearts. Forgiveness removes them.

Forgiveness releases resentments, hurt, pain, and stressful emotions, thereby erasing negative associations from the holographic field of the heart. Nonforgiveness can lead to hate that damages the heart emotionally, contracts it electrically, and pollutes spiritually.

In tuning in to positive frequencies, we move back into the flow of our lives. We create a new standard—one that is based on our own inner truth rather than an outside, arbitrary "truth." Empowered by deepening awareness, we are no longer dependent on others for validation and approval. We free both ourselves and others to be who we are. We begin to see ourselves as essence. As well, we can see the essence within others, regardless of outer appearances.

THE HIGHER HEART FREQUENCIES

Heart frequencies are feelings, and feelings are what makes life worthwhile. Higher heart vibrations are the higher aspects of human nature—serenity, laughter, love, compassion, forgiveness, tolerance, gratitude, appreciation, kindness. These are "in sync" with core values. These frequencies are accessed from the core, meaning the heart. The primary feeling is simply unconditional love.

The higher heart bands are a bridge into the field of essence. They are the highways of divine energy. Accessing these higher bands regenerates the immune system. They're in charge of the fountain of youth. Our "ageless body" resides in the higher frequencies.

The way to tune in to love is to connect with our hearts at the deepest level. In any situation, phrases such as "I am present in the moment," "Stay in the heart," and "Open the heart" are useful techniques for grounding ourselves on the path of the heart. If we feel ourselves closing down, freezing, turning off, erecting a defensive wall, we can consciously remind ourselves in this way of the path of heart. If we feel afraid, depressed, irritable; if things aren't going our way in a meeting with a client; if we're frustrated by a creative logjam, we can return to the source of "flow" by silently repeating words like these.

As well, taking a deep breath is always helpful. We can imagine that we are breathing in the luminous golden light of the higher frequencies and that we ourselves are dissolving into that flowing, nectarlike energy of love.

Love serves as the ultimate healer because it keeps our hearts and heads in balance.

THE MIDDLE HEART FREQUENCIES

The middle emotions on our frequency band are sentimentality, expectations, attachments, desires, sympathy, and pity. These are somewhat neutral in affect, depending on how we use them. That quality makes them tricky.

These emotions are challenging fodder for inner work. With awareness, they can be used as a road in to the higher frequencies. Without awareness, they can draw us in to a web of negative emotions.

For example, when love turns into attachment, or compassion gets colored by sympathy, the heart-energy condenses into sadness or pain. We become "heavy-hearted." We feel disappointed, and we keep replaying our sad old movie, reinforcing the hurt feelings each time we do so. But in truth a broken heart is a head-on collision between middle heart frequencies and higher heart frequencies.

We loved, but the love drifted to the middle heart frequency, where it became expectation and attachment. If we have the inner awareness to see what has happened, our disappointment can become a path to liberation. We can rejoice in our ability to love, in our longing to love, in our love itself. We can release our pain and move on.

Particularly if we have been victims of traumatic abuse, we might need to access some other higher-frequency feelings to help us move along the path of heart. Forgiveness, for example—of ourselves first, and then of others—can often pave the way to releasing self-pity.

Real love is caring and forgiving. It transcends even the limitations we make up in the name of love. If we can find a way to transform attachment into unconditional love, or pity into compassion, our heart-energy is enlightened. We feel "light-hearted."

As well, we can align ourselves with wholesome desires. We can channel desire into ardently wishing that everyone reside in the resonance of the heart. Then obviously we are tuning in to the higher frequencies.

THE LOWER HEART FREQUENCIES

The negative emotions are anger, fear, depression, apathy, boredom, anxiety, irritation, frustration, exhaustion, low self-esteem, unfulfillment, tension, discouragement, and stress reactions. When we solidify these, we cut off our connection with the world of essence.

However, just because emotions like anger, fear, apathy, sadness, and so on vibrate at lower frequencies doesn't mean that we should turn away from them when they arise. Before we can productively work with negative emotions, we must allow ourselves to feel their energy fully.

When we identify with negative emotions, they increase our sense of separateness. However, when we allow ourselves to experience them fully by moving *toward* them, they can be extremely useful as we continue to journey on the healing path of heart. Connecting with these negative emotions in ourselves and feeling them leads to compassion and lovingkindness for ourselves. Working creatively with them can bring us back to higher-frequency feelings. Knowing them leads to knowing ourselves.

Unless we feel compassion for our pain, we will not know how to extend lovingkindness toward ourselves. And unless we know ourselves fully and are able to feel compassion and lovingkindness toward our own being, we can never extend ourselves toward or understand others. As we shall see in the following chapters, being there for others, in relationship and service, is the next step on the healing path of heart. In the big story, *all* emotions are part of the human experience. We don't have to beat ourselves up for experiencing a negative emotion—

which so often takes the form of reinforcing our negative story line or retreating into addictive behavior.

Negative circumstances offer a great opportunity to see ourselves in the third dimension as a healing instrument. Even when we are in pain, we can use whatever we encounter to rise into a higher consciousness and emanate healing energy into the world.

Flipping Negative Emotions into Positive Ones

A simple way to drop our attachment to negative situations and expand into the higher frequencies is to attach ourselves to something more positive. Our entire energy system is more efficient when we learn to "time out" negative mental imagery, surrender to heaven and earth, and then actively embrace a positive image.

As the Lakota say, "Illness cracks us open to mystery."

Years ago I was having dinner with Norman Cousins in Los Angeles. We talked a lot about his famous recovery from ankylosing spondylitis (a disintegration of the connective tissue in and around the spinal column), as recounted in his book *Anatomy of an Illness*. He told me in detail how he laughed at his diagnosis of terminal disease, giving rise to an exhilaration attack that shifted the focus of his whole life and set him on a course of action. As he was healing, he actively cultivated the higher heart frequency of humor. His therapy included, for example, watching Marx Brothers movies and anything else that would make him laugh. What he experienced not only healed him, he also ended up being the only non-medical doctor on the faculty at the UCLA center for research into psychoneuroimmunology. His healing approach, as detailed in the many books that followed, continues to have a positive influence on individuals and on research into fourth-dimensional—or transpersonal—healing.

Norman Cousins's experience is a perfect example of the interdimensional quality of the healing experience. In terms of the healing pyramid, he took responsibility for the healing method he chose and empowered his treatment with love, compassion, and forgiveness.

Moving Toward Negative Emotions

Working with our own pain and negativity allows us to develop skills for dealing with problems from a higher perspective. We can move bravely toward our negative emotions. There is no way we can know courage without knowing fear, no way to know confidence without knowing doubt, no way to know peace without knowing war.

We can also offer our lower-frequency feelings. We can offer them to ourselves, to ghosts, to gods, or to other human beings.

To offer them to ourselves, we can simply allow these emotions to be in our world. We do not resist them; we do not push them away. Allowing a negative emotion to be in our world can enable us to transform it into positive action. We can wear it as an ornament.

For example, the Dalai Lama does not hate the Chinese Communists who overran his country in 1959, killing monks and laypeople, destroying monasteries, and driving hundreds of thousands of Tibetans into India as refugees. However, he's very angry with them. He is not holding *on* to anger, he *has* anger. Anger is something that occurs in his emotional territory. He has anger, and at the same time he travels throughout the world calling attention to the plight of Tibet. He is engaging his feeling in a proactive way.

We can offer our negative emotions to gods as well. Surely we have all made deals with God. When I was about nine years old, my beloved grandpa, who was about ninety, called the family together. First he blessed us all (he was a very pious man) and then he said, "The Lord is calling." I shouted, "Oh no!" Obviously, I did not want him to go.

That night when I went to bed, I made a deal with God. I told God, "God, I don't want my grandpa to leave, but since you are all-powerful, I will chew a stick of gum all night as a sacrifice. And through this sacrifice, you will keep my grandpa alive." I was offering up my resistance in the form of a stick of gum. Don't we all make deals with God? And does God keep his side of the promise that he never agreed to? Absolutely not!

Later that night Grandpa said again, "The Lord is calling," closed his eyes, and left. The next morning I knew he was gone, because the house was very quiet and my mother was wearing black. I knew he wasn't there. I was nine years old and very disappointed with God, who had failed. What a gift! My concept of God blew apart. What I mean by this is that my concept of transactional God— God as "Big Daddy"—blew apart. I was disappointed, but I learned the lesson of my life. You don't strike small story deals with God.

Everyone in the family was very depressed. We missed Grandpa terribly. The next night I had a dream. My grandfather came out of a tunnel of light and said, "Don't worry, we're fine, we're saved." Seeing my grandpa and hearing this message was wonderful. When I awoke, I felt ecstatic. I could hardly wait to tell my mother and my father. I thought it would make them feel as happy as it made me. But when I told them what I had seen and heard, they looked at each other and said, "Don't say that in public!"

My father had a black Underwood typewriter on which

I then typed a letter to my uncle: "Grandpa came and told me we're doing fine, don't worry." My uncle proceeded to give me positive feedback. He invited me for tea beside a beautiful swimming pool on the rooftop of an elegant hotel in Santiago. We sat down and he said, "Tell me about it." So I told him. He gave me chocolates and pastry. I got positive reinforcement for interdimensional perception.

I had been told, "Don't say that in public," so I didn't speak about it; instead I wrote my uncle about it. I wrote him a letter and he gave me a reward and listened to me. And it helped him in his healing process to know that we are eternal.

We can also offer our negative emotions to others. It helps us to feel connected to others, and it also helps them. His Holiness the Dalai Lama suggests that when we feel pained we imagine ourselves in someone else's shoes, visualize our pain as being theirs, and take it all on for their benefit.

As a psychiatrist, I remind patients who are in emotional pain and dysfunction that pain can be a compassionate aspect of our mission as human beings. As essential beings, perhaps we place ourselves in painful circumstances for the very reason that before we are able to resonate with the morphic field of others who are experiencing similar pain, we must first experience it ourselves. Whether or not our pain has some karmic or missionary aspect, we are definitely able to use it to make a heart connection with others.

Imagery

Imagery can also be an effective way of connecting with essence through negative emotions. It is important to first surrender to heaven and earth before practicing imagery like this. Through surrendering, we acknowledge the present moment as sacred space.

For example, we may feel anger. We can take a deep breath and feel the open space around ourselves. Now we can imagine our anger as a sharp, red-hot sword. We can muster all the aggression and anger we feel and empower the sword with it. Then we can visualize ourselves using the sword to puncture our ego-bubble and put us in direct contact with the world at hand.

Here is a more direct way to offer our negativity. In this instance, let's say we feel bleakly depressed because our marriage is dissolving. Again, we first surrender to heaven and earth. Then we conjure up the mental image of someone for whom we care deeply—for example, our child, our mother, our best friend—and imagine that he or she is depressed. Now we can visualize breathing in all that person's depression in the form of a giant black cloud. After that, we visualize breathing out an enormous golden cloud of joy, freedom from depression, or whatever we have to offer.

As we continue to do this, we can imagine more and more depressed people standing in front of us, and we can imagine our golden cloud of joy getting bigger and bigger. We can even imagine all the people in the world standing in front of us, and imagine our golden cloud permeating the universe. We can say a prayer, "May the depression that I feel encompass all the depression on earth. May no one be depressed but myself. May everyone else's depression be contained in me." It sounds as if this practice would increase depression, but remarkably, it has the opposite effect. Perhaps it works that way because in taking on others' depression we automatically widen our circle, and our personal pain feels smaller as a result. In any case, this is an extremely effective practice in helping to lighten our own pain and that of others.

If this seems like too big a job, we can use the same technique without visualizing others. We can breathe in our own depression and then, as we exhale, send ourselves whatever might cheer us up: for example, a bouquet of flowers, lovingkindness, or simply a stream of golden light.

We might not ever come into direct physical contact with others who are in the same kind of pain as we are. Yet when we feel a negative emotion and then lighten it up, we are performing a compassionate action. When we lighten it up, we vibrate a higher frequency that touches thousands of people having the same problem.

Offering is also a way to approach illness. In Tibetan Buddhism a practice called "offering to the ghosts" involves offering all one's negativity to whatever one fears. This exercise helps a person rise above the lower emotional frequencies into the greater reality of essence.

In this practice we might say a prayer such as, "If it benefits myself and others for me to be sick, let me be sick. If it benefits myself and others for me to recover, let me recover. If it benefits myself and others for me to die, let me die."

We might even say to our illness, "Thank you for causing me harm, and I invite you to return. Please take whatever you want—ravage me. I thank you for waking me up from my state of sleepiness and stupor." Thus, we acknowledge our gratitude for anything that wakes us up. This is a powerful way to go beyond clinging to hope and fear.

Mount Shasta

Several years ago I found myself camping overnight at Mount Shasta, an immense, mysterious mountain in northern California. At a transpersonal psychology conference, I had encountered a man whom I recognized as being from the brotherhood of those who realize themselves as souls. He asked me to come stay with him. That night I dreamed of a luminous old man with long hair—like God might look in our imaginations. So I decided to go. As I made the six-hour drive from San Francisco, I had a curious vision of this same being on top of the mountain.

Before I knew it, I was climbing up Mount Shasta with a backpack. I had a third-dimensional feeling of fragility. I'm not trained to climb high mountains, not trained to carry a backpack. I felt tired. This feeling brought me to a stage of perception at which I saw how impermanent everything is. Suddenly I was aware of the waves of the sea and how the sun was moving and how the colors were changing and how the leaves were falling. Everything was turning, like a living chain of events.

I found that if I focused on my perceptions, my mind dissolved, because each perception was going and coming and coming and gone. So I started doing a walking meditation. Now I found myself looking at what surrounded me from the iron perspective of the present moment. The grass, the trees, the sky—their colors, smells, and movements seemed so vivid and real. I sat down in the meadow where I would camp. There was a green field and some trees, and behind the trees was the forest. I could see the top of a snow-capped mountain.

I ate, and then I meditated some more. My meditation took me quickly from the third to the fourth dimension, then from the fourth to the fifth. Suddenly I knew that I was pure light.

At that moment I saw a mountain lion standing a few feet away. My hair stood up. I froze in fear. Without any thought, I just froze. The adrenaline, the heartbeat, the sweat engulfed me. I closed my eyes and continued meditating.

A fraction of a second later, it occurred to me that if I am light, all is light. The lion is light. I was very afraid. But if he ate me, it would be light devouring light, and we would be the same. I continued to experience the light, the bliss, and the joy. My body began to calm down. I was now handling this fear from a different place, but I was still concerned by the thought of what was going to happen. I opened my eyes again, staring at the lion. I smiled and recalled for a moment that life is light, that all that can happen is more light. I know somehow I connected with that lion and the lion knew it. After a short while, he ambled away into the forest.

Divine Direct Dialing

Emotions allow us to accept ourselves in all our perfect imperfection. We can accept ourselves in humility. We can forgive ourselves. We can embrace ourselves as who we are and what we have to work with. We can offer ourselves up.

In other words, we can choose to remember who we are and transmute whatever arises into higher frequencies.

Think for a moment about this: if we aspire not to limit what is limitless—not to condition what is unconditional—we will enter bigger and bigger space. That aspiration in itself becomes like jet fuel on the path of heart. It keeps us going, propels us forward. It allows us to face everything in our lives. We are willing to be courageous enough to face anything that arises.

We accept anything that happens to us as part of the human experience. We don't try to sweep anything under the rug. We have the power to transform it. The path of heart involves embracing the totality of the human experience, which is, after all, our own. We take the complete spectrum of the human experience as our working basis on the path of heart. When we take this healing attitude, anything that arises in our experience becomes an opportunity for treading further—not because the world is different, but because we are different.

The goal of treading the path of heart is to establish ourselves in Christ-consciousness. Whatever technique enables us to reach that goal, that's our path. All techniques work when we are devoted to the aspiration to go beyond ourselves and be of service.

When we commit ourselves to inner work and letting it transform our being, we don't look to others for confirmation. As the Sufi mystic Hazrat Inayat Khan said, "To every question that arises in the heart of the mystic he finds the answer in the life before him."

For our age, achieving Christ-consciousness might work through "DDD"—Divine Direct Dialing. Why? Because we're in a state of emergency. We have to wake up. We can do it because we must do it. And after we do it, the world will become larger. The reason that all traditions have the potential to work is that every single teaching in their inner sanctum is a means toward the same end.

We walk up the stairway of Kabbalah and we come out at the unnamable one, and we forget about the stairway. We sit at the *bodhi* tree of Buddhism and we become enlightened. We forget about the tree. When we practice properly, we dissolve. Once we dissolve, we reintegrate at a higher vibratory frequency, a new dimension of being.

❖ **EXERCISE** ❖

LISTENING TO THE HEARTBEAT AND
REMEMBERING THE MOTHER LINEAGE

In a quiet place where you will not be interrupted, lie down on the floor and surrender to heaven and earth by letting the floor support you. When your body and mind feel totally relaxed, tune your consciousness in to your heartbeat.

Entraining your mind with your heartbeat, now imagine that with each beat your heart emits waves of light. Relax there and entrain your mind with the waves of light. Now look into these waves of light and imagine that you see the face of your mother in those waves. Every time your heart beats, you see a wave of light, and in it the face of your mother.

Now continue to focus on your heartbeat and the face of your mother, and imagine that her mother joins her in that light. Then imagine that her mother's mother and her mother's mother's mother join them in that light. Now imagine that all the mothers in your lineage, which goes all the way back to Eve, are smiling at you from that particle of light. Now imagine that all sentient beings in the universe have been your mother and that they're all smiling at you from that particle of light. Imagine that all their heartbeats are beating with yours, all at once.

Now, smile back. Rest in the energy of your inherent goodness and intelligence, and that of all sentient beings, who have been your mother.

PART THREE

❖

The Face of the Divine Shines in Others

CHAPTER NINE

❖

Making Healing Energy Available in Relationships

As we learn to integrate higher frequencies of the heart, we will experience major shifts and changes in our perception. The perception of the heart—which is really heart and mind joined—is a holographic feeling-awareness that extends far beyond our bodies. The quality of this perception is sensitive, vivid, and real. It is with this open awareness that we experience the physical reality of interconnection with others and with everything else around us.

Physiologically, awakening our hearts also rouses parts of our brains that have been dormant. As these parts start to work, we may experience heightened intuition, synchronicity, extrasensory perception, or mental telepathy.

As our perception expands, it is possible to become stuck in the "trap of phenomena." Clairaudience, clairvoyance, and channeling are all considered lower psychic phenomena by spiritual teachers. As we awaken to essence, these symptoms appear as part of our development. In the West, we are so unused to these inner flows that we are prone to becoming obsessed by analyzing or pursuing them. We get stuck. If we can allow them to flow, however, our perception of ourselves and the surrounding world will open. Just as children learn to discriminate between colors, it is a natural progression.

When I was in India years ago, my teachers said it is important to say "No" to phenomena. Westerners have a propensity to get stuck on the idea of extrasensory perception, or ESP. Since our scientific conditioning denies ESP, it becomes very special to us when we begin to sense that it exists. What my Indian teachers knew is that this realm is not "extra." It's simply perception.

Imagine a five-year-old saying, "Blue, blue, blue," captivated by fascination as he learns to discriminate colors. That's the pitfall that awaits us as adults when we open our eyes to the fourth dimension. We rush around saying, "Yes, telekinesis exists! Prayer works!" We write books on the subject. We get bogged down in trying to prove the obvious, because science has convinced us that unless we can "prove" the existence of what we perceive, it cannot be true.

A woman I met at a conference, for example, was having a terrible relationship with her lover. She claimed to be channeling a fourth-dimensional entity who was telling her what to do. Because of what the entity was telling her, she'd stopped making love with her lover. Because she was strongly identified with this "angel," which might even have been her own ego, she could not see that by depriving her lover of sex, she was manipulating him. And her lover, a virile, healthy guy, was wilting like a plant without water.

The point is not to channel angels, but to channel love. Rather than becoming captivated by the fourth-dimensional world that is now revealing itself, we can continue to dwell in the opening heart.

The open heart is the garden in which the medicinal plants of core values grow. These plants include love, forgiveness, compassion, empathy, and many other qualities that we will discuss in the following pages. Our relationships with others provide a fertile opportunity for these qualities to thrive and bloom.

In the next three chapters I'm going to focus on a few obvious relationships: love relationships, work relationships, and parent-child relationships. But the tools and techniques I mention here can be used in all relationships. We do not have to limit our working basis on the path of heart to intimate relationships or work relationships. Even smiling at someone on the bus can be an expression of our open heart. Indeed, every person we meet is capable of enriching our lives. Everyone is a teacher, and we should honor them as such.

Many years ago in the midst of the military dictatorship in Chile, through the Drop of Honey organization we held a Day of Communication. The publicity campaign for this day was, "Act for one day as if whomever you encounter is someone you know. When you go into the subway, greet people. Look people in the eyes on the street because there's no threat." This is so contrary to how we are conditioned to act with strangers that we didn't have to worry about it becoming a habit. We encouraged people to do it for just one day.

People met. People met in the remembrance of love, of affinity, of contact. And they let down the barriers that we imagine stand between us. The surprising result of this Day of Communication was that the unemployment rate went down for that month, because people communicated and became more aware of each other.

Creating Healing Relationships

We can practice a medicine built on relationships. When we are devoted to moving toward greater awareness, the healing energy of core values is always available. As we work with others, we also enrich our own journey toward essential identity. In addition, our openness and wakefulness serve to help others wake up. As we become more skillful at using the resources of our open hearts, we can recognize relationships as training grounds for larger planetary service.

Healing ourselves involves learning to align with higher frequencies. And healing ourselves leads to healing others. Healing others leads to healing our families. Healing our families leads to healing community. Healing community leads to healing the earth. Healing the earth leads to healing ourselves. When we act from core values (as opposed to habit energy) the circular energy of the healing process opens itself to us, as we have opened our hearts to it. This energy exists only in the present moment. The abundance of the present moment is all we have, and it never ends.

If we were to realize our sacredness and know that we're in this forever, whether we imagine past lives repeating themselves or we think of never dying, wouldn't we construct a relationship that is safe, secure, and loving? Yes, of course.

THE VALUE OF INTIMATE RELATIONSHIPS

Relationships provide extremely fertile ground for the cultivation of core values. Relationships begin at home. We can start by taking a good look at our relationships with our intimates: parents, lovers, spouses, children.

Do these relationships bring us peace and love? Or are they sources of misery and pain? In particular, relationships that seem to keep us bound in pain should be explored. We must bring the light of essential identity to focus on their dark zones.

Our day-to-day relationships are rooted in domestic ritual, so they can easily become bound up by habitual pattern. However, as in the movie *Groundhog Day*, when Bill Murray keeps awakening to the same day over and over, the clock of our domestic routines offers us repeated opportunities to approach the same situations from a different angle. They invite our healing energy. Because we tend to think that our outer responsibilities hold greater importance, the daily dramas on the home front are also good practice for our appearances on a larger stage.

One reason why practicing treading the path of heart at home can be so interesting is that we all know how to push each others' buttons. Lots of juicy little negative feelings are always arising. At the same time, these often become inflated into negative emotions. Unless we consciously bring these lower frequencies to the path of heart by transforming them, they will block our hearts, creating defenses against love, peace, and expansion. This results in "unfinished business," which may manifest as illness.

For example, I knew a woman in her forties who became involved with a married man. She did not realize that his relationship with alcohol was fueling the "love" he professed for her. She fell hopelessly in love with him, and when he stopped seeing her, she became both depressed and obsessed. Shortly thereafter she was diagnosed with melanoma, which ravaged her totally, and three months later she was dead. To this day, her friends wonder about the relationship between her suppressed passion and her illness.

What we suffer when our intimate relationships are blocked by habitual reactions is what Mother Teresa called spiritual deprivation. Spiritual deprivation at home leads to unhealthy relationships with ourselves, the earth, and the cosmos. How can we care for the earth if we have not healed the misunderstandings of the past? How can we heal future generations if we live in fear and isolation?

How can we regard each moment as sacred space if we do not regard our homes as cathedrals, and ourselves and our families as divine?

RESPONSIBILITY, EMPATHY, AND FORGIVENESS

Blame and shame in particular can be enormous blocks in any relationship. They are inevitably rooted in the past. We cannot undo the past. However, we can undo our shame-based or blame-based attachment to it.

The antidote for blame and shame is, first, *responsibility*. Whatever the problem in our relationship is, we must take responsibility for it. We must recognize that others do not cause it; our perceptions, thoughts, and attitudes cause it.

The second antidote for blame is *empathy*. Empathy is feeling-in-other. We are so accustomed to feeling-in-ourselves that empathy might be the plant in our garden that requires the most intensive cultivation. Luckily, there are infinite opportunities to practice it. Recently, a friend of mine watched the entire four-movie series of *Jaws* from the perspective of the shark. She said that all the terror she experienced in watching it from her own perspective dissolved in this new way of seeing. That's empathy.

Essentially, empathy entails putting ourselves in the other person's shoes. This requires first "timing out" any negative mental images we might be carrying. Then we can begin to imagine how things are from the other person's perspective. If we center ourselves in the holographic feeling-awareness of the heart, we'll be able to sense that most of the time the other person isn't acting from malice—he's acting from blind reaction rooted in fear, insecurity, or any number of other negative emotions. Like the sharks in *Jaws*, most often he's acting out of hunger or fear. When we center ourselves in the heart, we can feel his pain.

In an emotionally charged situation, feeling someone else's pain cuts our own blind reaction. We don't have to get revenge. In fact, we can try to engender a sense of space in our relationship in which the other person might connect with his own pain. We can make a bridge of understanding with kind, accepting, and supportive words. We can even adopt the other's pain as our own by visualizing ourselves inhaling it as thick, black energy, and exhaling lightwaves of whatever that person seems to need—love, recognition, or simply space.

The third antidote to blame is *forgiveness*. Even if we've "walked a mile in someone else's moccasins," we may still feel that she is wrong in how she is acting toward us. If we are blaming ourselves, we feel shame. If we are blaming others, we feel blame. Think of the times that you have felt blame or shame, and you will see that these are emotions that take root and grow. By the time we see their full flower, they are completely rooted in the soil of the past.

When we recognize that blame and shame have their roots in the past, we can open to the present moment. This is the moment in which our hearts beat and divine energy is available to us. Using our inner awareness as a stepping-stone, we can forgive what has happened in the past. Forgiveness is the bridge to compassion. Compassion involves seeing pain and wanting to relieve it. It is a completely different space from blame and shame, in which we are referring backwards. Compassion is always available in the present moment; like essence, it is an energy that takes us forward into the service of others.

By forgiving ourselves and others we can continue to open our hearts. Forgiveness is a way of cleaning the slate. It severs past ties and puts our relationship squarely back into the present. Forgiveness oils the wheels of any relationship: without it, we grow further away from the other person instead of closer.

Forgiveness is the key to development in the pyramid of healing. Forgiveness vaporizes the blocks of limited third-dimensional perception so that we can love again. It resonates with other core values and activates the healing energy that abides in our hearts.

LEAVING MOM AND DAD BEHIND

One of the most intimate of all relationships is our relationship with our internalized parents. These manifest as voices in our heads that echo what our parents told us as we were growing up: "Don't ever run in public," "You look terrible in green," "I wish you were as good at math as Freddie"—these are just a few of the more harmless statements the voices might make. Many of our negative story lines come straight from our childhood experiences. It doesn't really matter what they are. On a grander scale, most of us adopt a personality structure that either reflects or rejects our parents' traits. When we begin to practice inner awareness, we might be faced with feeling blame or shame toward our parents for the "negative love" we may have suffered at their well-meaning hands.

As our hearts open, it is easy to become involved in what can become the time-consuming task of clarifying and straightening out our childhood traumas. Feeling abused or victimized by our parents has the ripe potential to become a nafs. Becoming identified with working it out is a false identification of who one is and can lead to endless loops of the same. Concurrently, it is important to acknowledge that even with the most loving parents, most of us were wounded as children—simply by virtue of miscommunication or misunderstanding, if nothing else. What we don't know, we need to find out. But finding out does not have to be a long process, since intrinsically we do know when we no longer deny our wound. Most of us are adult children of parents who forgot their essential identity.

The childhood wound becomes a filter through which we perceive the world. It is certainly helpful to know the character of the wound. What are its qualities? Do we habitually feel unloved, abandoned, left out? Or do we always feel like a failure? Without awareness and transformation, this wound will color all our relationships. But we don't have to spend years in therapy trying to work it out. As a therapist, I can tell you that I can "shrink" the process of therapy instead of my clients. I have discovered that in a very short time we can do a lot of work if we set the boundaries in many different dimensions. The process that I have developed, which I call the Psychospiritual Integration Process (PIP), introduces a deep clearing of early childhood problems in a minimum amount of time.

I conduct this therapy in intensive workshops that are carefully structured. We work on behavior patterns learned from parents that have blocked our personal development, and I present methods to overcome these negative attachments and dependency on external approval. In addition, the fifteen to thirty people who participate in each session learn how to turn to their inner self as the source of their own power, love, and well-being. Each workshop lasts nine days, and each participant does transmutation reprogramming "homework" for a year after that.

If we are genuinely committed to the path of heart, often we can work with healing this wound by ourselves on an ongoing basis. It helps to imagine our parents telling us who we are in the most positive terms. "Robert, who you are is essence, the purest, brightest stream of love. You have taken on this body in order to perform a unique service. Although it is necessary in this dimension to have a name and to learn some basic skills for making your way in the world and getting along with others, it is important to know that your true purpose here is to bring light into matter, and we are here to help you."

Then we can remember the times when our parents expressed love, concern, and support in positive ways. For our negative memories and feelings, we can practice substituting positive, happy memories of feeling valued and loved.

We can then accept our parents, empathize with them, try to understand them. Even more important, we can feel grateful for the life that came through them. We can wholeheartedly forgive them. And then, in a heartfelt way, we can take our leave.

LONELINESS

Yet another important factor in keeping any relationship flowing is slightly paradoxical: even though everything in the universe is interconnected, we must acknowledge that as individuals we are essentially alone. The innermost hollows of our being—while connected to essence—are accessible only to ourselves. Thus, we can't expect someone else to provide for us what only we ourselves can provide.

If we see that we are using a relationship to meet our personal needs, to further selfish interests, to gain sexual fulfillment, to reinforce who we "think" we are—as instant gratification, or to supply us with love at all times—we need to shift our perspective. If it is interesting to us, we can look at our expectations and see where they are rooted. Are we trying to attract something from the outside that is lacking within? Are we trying to push something away, perhaps because it scares us? Or are we trying to use the relationship simply as a way to keep ourselves asleep? When we have expectations, they are usually rooted in one of those motivations. Knowing where our expectations are rooted is the first step in working with them.

The energy to liberate expectations is always available in the present moment. Surrendering to the energy of heaven and earth, we can center in the heart. Taking a deep breath, we can then consciously expel the false identification and expectation that we have brought to our relationship. Inhaling, we can imagine the golden light of divine energy, essence, infusing our bodies. Then we can breathe that light out, visualizing it traveling to the other person.

We can make this exercise as specific as we wish. If we

find ourselves trying to control someone because we want them to love us, we can first recognize that we are attempting to attract from outside what is available to us within—love. Taking a deep breath, we can exhale our desire for love; when we inhale, we can imagine breathing in love from the vast ocean of divine love that surrounds us. We can say to ourselves, "All the love that I need is immediately available to me." We can imagine love filling our bodies. Then as we breathe out, we can say a prayer that the other person and every other being might know that all the love they need is always here. We can send them the golden light of divine love. We can continue to circulate love through our hearts whenever we think of it, offering its healing energy to ourselves and others.

True relationship comes not from expectation and the limitations of control, but from a coherent frequency of love. This is a higher energy than anger, greed, fear, or ignorance. When we tune in to this frequency, we can see ourselves from a clear place—the perspective of essence. Of course, then we can also recognize others from this point of view. We are more than solid material beings locked into false identifications, and so are others. In relationships, it is very important to stabilize this view.

When we abandon temporary identities and tread the path of heart, we can practice shifting our focus from interpersonal politics (which basically come down to, "Here's what I want, can you give it to me?") to the warm, pulsating, timeless space between heartbeats. This is a way to bring the healing energy of unconditional love into any relationship. In that unifying field, we recognize the essence of self and other.

Six Tools for Relating with Others

In the Buddhist tradition, there are six qualities known in Sanskrit as *paramitas,* which means "other shore." The "other shore" is the world that lies beyond the self. Traditionally, practicing these six virtues has been a way out of the ego realm and into the larger realm of enlightenment or essence.

Like responsibility, empathy, and forgiveness, these qualities are not only helpful but necessary in mobilizing us on the path of the heart. They include generosity, discipline, patience, exertion, wisdom, and awareness.

Generosity is a tool with limitless depth. When we feel like closing our hearts, generosity can take us beyond fear and help us keep them open. Thus, we extend generosity to ourselves. That allows us to extend generosity to others. One way of doing this is to offer ourselves to others. Offering ourselves to others is not limited to any particular form; it depends on the situation.

Our wisdom and awareness will show us what form might be appropriate. It might be physical offerings; it might take the form of simple, silent physical presence; it might involve taking time for a conversation; it might take the form of energy exchange with another person that involves sending them nonlocal medicine such as prayer or waves of light. The possibility for using generosity in working with others—even when we're alone—is limitless.

One teaching says, "Generosity is the virtue that produces peace." Try it and see if this is true.

Discipline is reflected in our commitment to tune in to the higher frequencies of the heart. We use whatever arises to make friends with ourselves, which allows us to make friends with others. This is lovingkindness.

Through our practice of inner awareness, we have tasted the seed of a larger world. Discipline continually transforms us into the proper container in which that seed will grow.

Patience means that we are willing to accept the abundance of the present moment as our open, groundless ground. The abundance of the present moment is enough. We want nothing more. Being a parent is a particularly rich situation in which patience is always helpful. In cultivating patience we can acknowledge that the way the world appears to us is not necessarily the way that it appears to others. Between a child and an adult, for example, the "vision gap" is particularly large.

Exertion means that we do not give up on ourselves, nor do we give up on others. Even when times are trying and we'd like to lazily burrow back into our cocoons, we must keep opening our hearts. We take joy in bringing whatever comes our way to the path of heart.

Wisdom involves discriminating in working with ourselves and others. We acknowledge that the present moment is always changing. What works in one situation might be utterly ineffective in the next. Wisdom acknowledges that every healing tool we have at our disposal is God-given and useful under the appropriate circumstances.

Awareness means taking responsibility for connecting with every facet of our world, and becoming totally involved in it. Awareness is the fuel that propels us toward the light.

The more we exercise virtues such as these to cultivate our awakening heart, the fewer desires we will have to return to sleep, because the life we will see awakened is beautiful. This beauty is crowned with love. That is the unity of all experience.

❖ **EXERCISE** ❖
CREATING A SACRED CIRCLE

Re-vision your home as a container for a sacred circle of love.

First, take one or two days to clean everything in your house. Whatever you don't need, make arrangements to sell it or give it to someone who needs it.

As you are cleaning your house, imagine yourself having a relationship with every object with which you come into contact. Wish every object well. Think of where it came from, who invented or created it, and how it is a manifestation of the innate intelligence, goodness, and compassion of its source.

Now turn to the people, animals, and plants that share your home. Imagine them as globes of golden light. Imagine yourself as a globe of light. Imagine that there are no boundaries between yourself and those who share your home. Imagine that all of you are emanating this light, and that you are all joined in it. Visualize it as filling your home. You are all bathed in the golden light of love, of compassion, of deep caring.

You can continue this visualization for as long as you want. A helpful thing to do in order to remind yourself that your home is a sacred place is to designate a small area in your kitchen, dining room, family room, or living room where you can put a flower or some other beautiful object, and perhaps burn a stick of incense from time to time. Make this an offering to your sacred circle.

CHAPTER TEN

❖

Romantic Love

Our cultural conditioning tells us, "Be normal." "Be like everyone else." "Wear the same kind of mental-emotional-psychological outfit as everyone else and you'll be accepted and loved." But are we loved? Are we accepted? Absolutely not. Because no one knows us.

I've had couples in therapy who say, "We've been married for forty years and I don't think he gets who I am, I don't think she gets who I am." Of course our spouse doesn't "get" who we are, because *we* don't "get" who we are! What we're emanating is pretense. What we're emanating is unreality. What we're emanating is a lie. If we're lucky, one day we wake up and look at this lie that is our life, and we say, "What am I doing here?" Well, for one thing, we are giving work to divorce attorneys, psychiatrists, cardiologists, and oncologists.

We hide in temporary identities. We hide our treasure—essential identity. Is our treasure too hidden to come out and resonate with the uniqueness of who we are? Can we drop our nafs and bring ourselves into the room?

The joke is, we already *are* in the room. We already *are* on the planet. We already *are* doing every single thing we have invented. We already *are* essence. But *we* aren't realizing who we are. We're hiding our jewel in a dustbin—as the Buddhists say—waiting in the hidden recesses of our consciousness to be discovered.

The moment we lost paradise is when we first thought of ourselves as separate beings. That's what the myth of Adam and Eve is all about. Adam and Eve discovering their nakedness and leaving Eden is a portrayal of the moment we perceive ourselves as separate. We leave the fifth-dimensional awareness of unity and fall into dualistic thinking. That's the moment we transfer the certainty of *being* a soul into having a soul. Once we have something, it becomes a possession. It can be taken from us, controlled, manipulated. Humanity has been asleep thinking that what we have can be stolen from us; what we *are* can never be stolen from us. Humanity has been asleep thinking that we have to do something to get our souls back; they've been right here all along. It's time to wake up!

We can use every experience in our lives to move toward essence. Romantic love is one of the most precious gifts in this regard. Love is a doorway through which we grow bigger. It is a universal energy that helps us evolve. Feeling a sense of union with another person gives us a microcosmic view of the unified field of the fifth dimension. We melt into it like butter.

Through romantic love we can see the face of the divine in one another. When we meet someone and feel that timeless shift of connection from heart to heart, from soul to soul, we say, "I want it to be forever." And inside we know we have already reached that place of "forever-ness"—because when we fall in love with someone, we always feel novelty and familiarity at the same time.

This feeling is to be trusted. I know of many happy examples. A dentist friend who was my client met his future wife when she was three years old and he was five. They married when she was nineteen. Now they're in their sixties, still sharing ongoing companionship, curiosity, and spiritual recognition. Their circle of love has widened to include three children and eight grandchildren.

Another man I know fell in love with a woman at college, but circumstances had it that they both married someone else. However, they kept up a correspondence. When both lost their spouses they got together at age sixty-four, their love as fresh as ever.

When I met my wife, Carolina, I experienced a fairly common phenomenon that is rarely talked about; it is sometimes called the quickening. We don't usually see it coming; it almost always takes us by surprise. It can come from the touching of two people's subtle bodies or energy fields.

This phenomenon is almost always accompanied by the positive frequencies of life, light, love, or laughter. It may be experienced somewhat differently by different people, but it usually comes with a sudden awareness or realization. Then we feel a speeding up of time and a rush of energy. It usually pushes us toward some course of action in tune with the new awareness.

When I experienced this feeling after being introduced to Carolina at a weekend workshop, I sublimated the impulse. Although in those days it was not unusual for me to be attracted to some of my students, I had learned to maintain boundaries appropriate to our roles. Since she was only eighteen years old and I was a ripe thirty-seven, I felt that my attraction might not be particularly appropriate. I was suspicious of it. For though sometimes the quickening is the "call of destiny," it can also distract us from our spiritual path or our purpose in life.

The next time I met Carolina I felt flushed, giddy, and excited to have another chance to see her. This time, I could not ignore my feelings. I felt a dreamy ecstasy in making eye contact with her that I had never felt with a student before. I felt like I was a teenager again, and that deepened excitement gave me the courage to consider trying to approach her.

It is popular these days to talk of "soulmates." When I think of a soulmate, I imagine someone who is complete in herself and with whom we can expand our own sense of completeness. There are certain territories of life and perception that are simply not accessible to a single individual. A soulmate serves as a complement, not a completion, to our lives and can help us expand into those new territories of experience. The extension of the "I" requires a true "Thou," as Martin Buber would say. I wondered if Carolina were my soulmate.

At another workshop some time later, we divided into smaller groups for discussion. As I made my rounds to each of the groups, I found myself in a small lounge with five students. There was Carolina. I was closer to her than I had been in weeks. But even in this context, I didn't feel comfortable sharing my feelings for her. During one of the exercises, though, she made her feelings clear. "I love you," she told me.

I had been told things like that by other women students in the past who were projecting all sorts of fantasies on me—from father to lover to saint—and so, as if by reflex, I responded in my usual therapeutic mode, "Do you love yourself?" I thought I detected an expression of surprise and disappointment cross Carolina's face, as if I doubted the sincerity of the love she felt for me.

The next morning's workshop session was run by my co-presenter. It included an exercise known as the "stop" exercise, developed by Gurdjieff. As music played, all the participants were asked to move about the room using their whole body. At several points during the movement exercises the leader shouts "Stop," and everyone freezes in the position they are in at that moment.

For the next minute or so, while everyone is holding their pose, the leader directs them to withdraw from their ego-consciousness and observe themselves from the detached perspective of their Inner Witness. The Inner Witness has the perspective that can observe what we're feeling, sensing, and thinking as we are stopped in a pose. Then the leader shouts "Go," and the participants are directed to relax their minds and move around to the music until they are frozen again.

Now when I lead this exercise, I direct students to shift their Inner Witness to their heart, in order to make sure they are in touch with a larger perspective and more coherent frequency before continuing. When we use this process, we achieve an ability to master our focus and concentration while we are actively engaged in something else. What we are doing is stabilizing our consciousness in essential identity, which doesn't depend on a specific action to nourish it. It is also a helpful process because the Inner Witness, among other things, can help us better identify and heal dysfunctions in our life and open us more fully to the interdimensional world.

As my co-presenter led the workshop participants

through this exercise, I realized that my mouth was hanging open in awe as I saw the graceful way Carolina moved with absolutely no self-consciousness. My heart wanted to jump out of my chest.

At the end of the workshop the next day, I held a ceremony I called my graduation address. I talked about the power of being and gave the participants "diplomas." I also gave small gifts to the various session leaders and coordinators as I acknowledged their contributions. After I had called everyone else in the room to the stage to receive something, I asked Carolina to approach the platform. I took her hand and placed in it a rose quartz crystal in the shape of a heart. At that moment, we accepted each other.

The first week Carolina and I were together it was as if images of our past lives floated past and cleared themselves from our minds so that we could be intensely, passionately, and wholeheartedly present. I couldn't begin to convey in writing the magnificence of feeling one in two bodies and knowing with total certainty all about each other's essence. What I felt was somehow beyond the mating of two souls. This was new to me.

Thus, how our relationship began was like a subtle dance in the warm pulsation of divine love. We allowed our magnetic attraction to arise and flow in this vast space before either of us articulated it. We bathed in the warmth of it. We didn't have to create the situation; it was there for us to watch, to dance with. When the moment of acceptance came, neither of us felt self-conscious as we relaxed into the abundance of our mutual creation. We allowed our spiritual attraction to unite us in the sanctity of matrimony and no words can even attempt to describe the echo of the sound of true union.

Love as a Sacred Circle

If we have eros, sex, and love in a romantic relationship, we are blessed with a situation that is very powerful for spiritual growth. Erotic love brings the work of God—the work of integral love—to its complement here on earth. Eros is a highly charged spark of divine energy.

The key to balancing the three elements is to keep our relationship flowing, and never let a doubt of our blessedness enter. We can accept our relationship as a gift, not as something we created. We can trust the gift. This keeps the mystery intact. We can regard our relationship as a sacred circle in which we practice core values.

In other words, we can use our union to open our hearts further and further.

One way we can do that is by having a commitment to the other person as essence, not as our perception of who they are. When we recognize the other as soul, we are also recognizing that our relationship is limitless and unconditional. Furthermore, we know that it is constantly changing. If we remain open to essence in ourselves and each other, the eros we feel has the capacity to reveal deeper and deeper layers of unified energy. New dimensions are always at hand. This encourages the expansion of eros.

If we are generous, we can even expand the eros we feel to those beyond our relationship. In continually offering our union to the divine, we model the living energy of eros. We can radiate to others the divine love that is channeled through our union. We can visualize our love benefiting others.

Eros provides a strong first momentum to connect with another person. Through years of being with them, exertion, generosity, forgiveness, empathy, patience, awareness, appreciation, wisdom, and discipline help to keep the relationship open and flowing. Approaching our relationship from this perspective protects us from some of the pitfalls and dangers of marriage. This is how we continually transform eros into true love.

The energy of true love has been known to cross even physical boundaries. For example, my grandparents were married for sixty years. The day my grandfather called the family together to bless us, he told my grandmother that he was going ahead and was not going to leave her behind for long. After he died, she would tearfully talk to him. Three months later to the day, she died.

I would hope that all of us have experienced eros at least once in our lives—that moment of excitement at discovering someone new or suddenly encountering a new aspect of someone we've known for a long time. The way it felt for me the first time I ever experienced it in a relationship was as a sense of wonder: I was constantly surprised and amazed at what the other said and did. Everything felt unexpected and fascinating. It was truly a voyage of discovery.

Keeping Eros Alive

My marriage continues to be like that. However, I see that it is very different in other relationships. We often begin to dislike our wives or husbands and label everything they do or say as "the same old stuff." In such cases we are denying ourselves the deep knowing that guides us to the new vistas available in any relationship. Unfortunately, it seems that we often don't want to see them. We become locked into the nafs of relationship. We see only what we want to see. This deadens us to the abundance of living energy that is available.

We might unconsciously agree on fixed images of each other. We do this out of a sense of fear or the need to be in control or a desire for security. We feel threatened. The deep trust available in a growing relationship is obstructed. When we paint a fixed picture of our lover in our minds and refuse to see anything that varies from that picture, we close down. We are able to see the outside, but we no longer see the inside depths of our partner. At the same time, we lock ourselves into our lover's image of us. Our relationship stops growing.

But if we are committed to the essence in each other, we keep revealing ourselves. No matter what is revealed, if it is revealed in honesty and openness, the love that grows is tangible. When we open ourselves deeply, we are loved. We are naturally drawn together. This is true eros—an interdimensionality of knowing another soul.

We hunger for that deeper connection, to truly know the other. The more we know, the stronger our appetite to know. Our revelation of ourselves to others has the same effect on them. This deeper way of knowing feeds us, supports us, and nurtures our ability to love. Our union grows, and so does our knowledge of the truth.

When such a relationship ends, we can carry the energy into another. I met a sixty-three-year-old woman whose husband had died three years earlier. They had had ten children. For forty-three years they were as in love as the day they had met, and they continued to be sexually active. She was deeply saddened at his passing, but nevertheless she had fallen in love again with his seventy-four-year-old partner, with whom she had been friends for a long time. Because she had had such a wonderful marriage before, she was going to marry again. "Unfortunately," she told me, "we won't have time to have children."

Using Obstacles to Enlarge the Sacred Circle

It isn't as if our union is without emotional texture. When we are committed to the viewpoint of essence, our sacred circle is big enough to contain whatever arises. We know that we are loved unconditionally. It's a safe, secure container in which to explore what we feel. The value of emotional upsets in strong relationships is precisely that they usually point us to unresolved issues or unfinished business.

Most heightened emotions represent the reactivation of unresolved pain from the past. We are rarely upset for the reason we think we are. There is always value in looking deeper. Our feelings are our teachers. They can act as springboards for personal and spiritual evolution to the fifth-dimensional self. Higher self always directs us to a place of greater love, power, and mastery.

At these times, opening to our partner will not always showcase our higher selves. Part of what we reveal to each other will be our lower selves, which we tend to hide as negativities, impurities, embarrassments. These are often elements that we actively dislike. Our partner may be the only person on earth in whom we feel enough trust to reveal these vulnerabilities, which make us feel raw and exposed. But by revealing what we would most like to keep hidden, we can help each other grow. Opening sparks eros.

MAKING FRIENDS WITH FEAR

The main obstacle to treading the path of heart with another is fear. When we experience fear, we might have the impulse to close off from our partner. Just as likely, we might try to control the situation. Here is an example of how we can use these threatening emotions to open our relationship further.

When fear, for example, arises, we can first imagine ourselves completely relaxing in our relationship. (If we're not in a relationship and have conflicting feelings about being in one, we can do this exercise by visualizing ourselves in the perfect relationship.) As we do this, we notice what feelings arise. As a feeling arises, we can listen to what it has to say. How does it feel threatened by our relationship? Why does it want to be separate?

We might try sharing this exercise with our partner. It is important that we share with self-responsibility; that is, not from blame or projecting feelings onto our partner. Rather, we claim our feelings as our own. It might sound something like this: "When I look at my desire to be more fully in union with you, a deep fear comes up. I'm afraid of losing myself in the relationship, of being swallowed up." Or, "When I feel fully in union with you, the mystery of it terrifies me. The energy is too big for me. So I feel the urge to somehow control it."

Often such sharing will call forth a similar feeling from our partners, and thus begins the dance of eros, in which we each take the risk of going deeper, revealing more. As we reveal more and pay attention to what is revealed, we see our partners as more honest, more real. Our hearts open again. Fear becomes trust. The need to control becomes renewed commitment to the path of heart.

Having said all that, I also should acknowledge that

not all of us are in a position to do this. We may find ourselves with a partner who is frightened of deep revelations—theirs or ours. Deepening a relationship can't be forced. But we can also try to take a step forward with the energy of the situation rather than feeling like a failure. We can try to look at our partner (or ourselves) with compassion and understand where we are, what our struggle is, and lend support, forgiveness, and gratitude.

Opening to the present moment is, as always, important. Is it frightening to reveal ourselves? Then we can sit with that fear and look at it. Is our fear real? Is what we feel truly fearful? Or is it old stuff that we don't need anymore? We can help our partner undergo a parallel exploration. We can ask what she is feeling, assure her that whatever it is, it is okay because it's what she is feeling in the moment. Then we can support her, wherever she is.

This is how we give each other the gift of our true selves. We continue to open to the limitless and unconditional nature of our gift. To practice true union, we must know ourselves first. A certain emotional and spiritual maturity has to come into play. If we are so fortunate as to be given this opportunity, we can consciously regard our union as a physical reflection of our personal unity, and of the unified field of the fifth dimension.

Gratitude

What kills eros after the honeymoon ends is the raft of projections, expectations, "shoulds," judgments, and demands that we make on each other. When eros is gone, we may feel that our basic needs are no longer being met. Frustration appears, and our love becomes conditioned by what we need. Our relationship becomes a trade-off: "I will love you if you will give me sex, money, status, security"—whatever it is we need. The spark of eros—which is one of the broadest, most abundant, and elaborate gateways to the fifth dimension—no longer seems available. So we look for third-dimensional (that is, material) ways to replace what has been lost.

From time to time I see couples in therapy who have locked horns over some issue or another and suffered a downward spiral to such lower depths. This dualistic trend can only be healed by love: it heals anxiety, irritability, doubt, worry, anger, and the entire negative band. At times like these, it may be helpful to unravel the interpersonal dynamics in the interest of casting the light of awareness into the dark zones. Becoming aware of the dysfunctions in our relationships is part of cultivating self-responsibility. I also try to encourage starting over with a clean slate by exhorting my clients to forgive themselves and each other.

But first it is most helpful for each member of the relationship to dedicate himself or herself to waking up the true essence of love, joy, and happiness within. This inevitably reduces the level of finger-pointing, blame, and expectation. When they find it in themselves to forgive their partner, doors of opportunity start to open. In the healing pyramid, forgiveness is the key to higher dimensions. I also encourage these couples to be grateful for each other, knowing that gratitude is another quality that has great power in cutting through negative habitual patterns in relationships.

To this end, some of the couples who come to see me leave with T-shirts that I prescribe. I instruct them to wear the T-shirts to bed. Then when they wake up in the morning, the first thing they see is the slogan on the other's T-shirt: "If I'm good enough for God, I'm good enough for you."

Another of my favorite prescriptions is to ask my clients to listen to each other with the "ear" at the center of the heart. Listening with our hearts inevitably helps us find the strength to recycle fear and frustration based on false identity and expectation into joy and fulfillment rooted in knowing ourselves and our partners as essence.

The greatest key is compassion, which mobilizes us in the pyramid toward the highest unification. Genuine compassion is not based on our projections and expectations but on the needs of the other person. As long as we wish to overcome suffering, then we develop genuine concern. We have to distinguish compassion from attachment. Marriages that last for a long time have, besides love, compassion for each other. After a moment of change, compassion emerges and our hearts open wider.

Compassion can emerge only when we know ourselves. Then we have the courage and the resources to cross from the illusory, time-bound third dimension into the timeless abundance of eros, divine love, and expanding awareness.

❈ EXERCISE ❈
THE CIRCLE OF LOVE

The next time you make love with your partner, try this. It will be an even more intense experience if your partner does the exercise at the same time, but for even one of you to practice it is satisfying.

As you begin to make love, envision a golden ball of light above the two of you. Now imagine the light descending into your heart, and into the heart of your lover. The two of you are suffused with light.

As your love-making intensifies, imagine the light traveling down from your heart to your genitals. At the moment of orgasm, imagine the light of your lover in union with yours. Now watch and feel as the light streams up from your genitals, into your heart, up into your head. It flows from your mind into the mind of your lover, streaming into his heart, down to his genitals, up through his genitals into yours, up into your heart, and so on. Enjoy this circle of light. Melt into its warmth, and rest in the joy of basic love and goodness.

CHAPTER ELEVEN

❧

In Service of the Sacred

There are many ordinary life events that serve as initiations into essential identity, if we will only surrender to them. Through them, we are awakened to a larger world. They automatically open our hearts and challenge us to keep them open.

One of the major life initiations that we experience is falling in love, which we have just discussed. The others are birth, illness, and death. Parenting and vocation are ongoing initiations that offer moment-by-moment inspiration for connection. All these events challenge us to "sacred service," providing us with the opportunity to serve others.

If we engage ourselves fully in these situations, we can use them to channel the divine energy that comes through our awakened hearts, and our own sense of sacred identity expands. As the Sufi sage Hazrat Inayat Khan said, "The essence of spirituality and mysticism is readiness to serve the person next to us."

Birth

If we have made a sacred circle of our relationship, we have established a strong container of heart awareness into which to welcome children. Parenting children is one of the most demanding and rewarding endeavors of human life. It opens new horizons in terms of keeping ourselves steadfastly treading the path of heart.

On the one hand, it presents ample new ways in which we can open our hearts day by day, minute by minute. On the other hand, it presents pressures that often invite us to close down. But even when we as parents close down, our vocation always opens us up again. The love that is inherent in parenting a child provides a door to connection that is open always. If we are committed to mindfulness of the present moment, that door keeps opening itself.

Conception and pregnancy are initiations into an enchanting dance of interconnection. A pregnant woman enters into a mysterious world where she is at the service of an unknown being. Concerns that before had been uppermost in her mind—career, the daily news, social obligations—begin to pale when compared to the miracle and mystery of the growing child inside her. Symptoms such as morning sickness and the general glow of pregnancy conspire in this most universal of initiations. It is as if in a very natural way the mother is obligated to put aside "self" for the benefit of another.

Pregnancy is not simply an introduction to selflessness—it can also be an initiation into the invisible worlds of the fourth and fifth dimensions. Dreams, intuitive feelings, and for some, communication with the unborn child are well-known phenomena. One of my students became ill about a week before she conceived her son. She was able to eat nothing, drink nothing, and do nothing except lie in bed in her darkened room. In this condition, she was drawn to a streak of white light that seemed to be zooming around the perimeters of the ceiling.

Of course, she chalked up her vision to hallucination owing to her illness. However, the first time she and her husband made love after she was feeling better, she saw the white light come down from the ceiling and felt it enter her body with a force so strong that it was, she says, "like being hit by a brick."

For myself and Carolina, the conception of our second child, Charlie, provides an interesting example of the living mystery. We were in the Dalai Lama's house in India. We didn't have any real plans for pregnancy because our daughter was only a few months old. Carolina was breastfeeding Alexandra, and I was having an ecstatic meeting with His Holiness. He was asking me how the Jews survived after the destruction of the temple two thousand years ago. This was important to him because his temple also has been destroyed—by the Chinese in 1959. And I was asking him about the continuum of consciousness that has no alpha and no omega, no beginning and no end.

Now picture the scene: it's India, it's the end of November, it's cold in the Himalayas. My general director for India who had organized workshops for me there is filming us with the cap on the lens, Carolina is breastfeeding Alexandra, I'm sitting back with my jacket on while His Holiness is laughing.

We'd been meeting for hours. Toward the end, I said, "Your Holiness, do you think I should become a monk?" He began to laugh and answered, "I'm the monk. You're the father. You should have a son." We went back to our room, which was very cold. We were sleeping dressed.

Carolina said, "If you want to conceive in India, it's to-day." So Charlie got a visa to the West.

Birth is also an initiation. As parents-to-be, we are encouraged to plan the birth, to imagine it just as we'd like it to be. We might plan a home birth, a midwife-assisted hospital birth, a waterbirth. Yet our preconceptions can stand in the way of the initiation that giving birth is. No matter how carefully we plan, we are not in charge. This is the next stage of the initiation.

When Carolina was pregnant with David-Gabriel, our youngest child, she bled from the beginning on. She had to lie in bed a lot. After I returned from a lecture tour to South America, I noticed that she looked pale when she picked me up at the airport. The next morning I took her to a hospital in Flagstaff, an hour away. Diagnosed with severe anemia, she needed a transfusion of eight units of blood. For three days she hovered between life and death. On Father's Day 1994 an emergency caesarean section had to be performed. Little David-Gabriel was born six months after conception, weighing less than two pounds.

Shortly after his birth I flew in a private plane with him from Flagstaff to Phoenix, where he was able to get the neonatal intensive care that he needed. He was in intensive care for twelve days. Meanwhile I was traveling a thousand-mile circuit between Phoenix, Sedona (to see my two other children), and Flagstaff, where Carolina was recovering. In Flagstaff I would pick up Carolina's breastmilk for David. In Phoenix I would feed him the milk and hold him on my chest for hours at a time, warming his little body kangaroo-style. Forty days later the baby was home and thriving. My heart was ecstatically grateful that David-Gabriel and Carolina were alive. His birth—so radically different from Alexandra's and Char-

lie's—reminded me that parenthood is a continual process of letting go of preconceptions about how life will
be.

Inviting Children to the Path of Heart

Becoming a parent is a precious gift. It offers us the opportunity to take our place in the lineage of the human
race. It provides us an ongoing occasion to transmit our
wisdom to others. It opens our hearts with gratitude
toward our parents and ancestors. In the eyes of our children, we see the future. It also provides a splendidly
wide, ever-changing horizon on which to continually
align ourselves with core values on the path of heart.

Where do our children come from? At birth, the child is
the picture of essence, unconditional love. The baby is
his own unique self. Before the baby comes we may be
full of schedules, routines, plans, and aspirations. But
when we hold the little one in our arms for the first time,
all our preconceptions are blown away like a leaf in the
wind. We fall into the wide-eyed wonder of the baby's
eyes and we're "theirs." But they are not "ours."

If we can wake up independently and see that who we
are is not a father or a mother, but a soul interacting with
another soul setting some rules, boundaries, and guidelines for third-dimensional operation and growth, we can
avoid the pitfalls of negative love. Negative love is the
most crippling disease in the universe. It imposes preconceptions, beliefs, judgments, and other forms of negative
control on our children. The child in her development
misreads and interprets these as love.

Thus, a girl who has been taught that she is loved
when she makes straight A's embarks on a lifetime of

unfulfilled perfectionism. A boy who is pushed into sports when what he loves is music is quickly pushed out of touch with his own needs and desires. In loving our children this way, we limit what is limitless and condition what is unconditional.

As parents we face an enormous responsibility. Many of us have had to pass through the arduous process of recovering our sacred identity, having been conditioned by negative love to forget it. Now we can pray for divine guidance in supporting, accepting, and guiding our children in recognition of their essential identity, so that they do not have to rediscover it. It is our responsibility to nourish their essence, to do nothing that would obscure it, and to do everything to further their connection with themselves. In nourishing our children, we nourish the human race.

The child is born with full-blown goodness and innate intelligence. Our job is to mirror those qualities, to provide the reflective environment in which they can grow. Our job is to model being human.

Children absorb everything that happens to them. Even with babies, our responsibility is to mirror core values in our interactions. Even a newborn knows whether it is being held with warmth, care, and tenderness, or in simply an offhand manner. It knows when its cries for food and companionship are truly heard. A baby who invites his mother into play knows when she is in a hurry or when her heart isn't in it.

Babies and children whose needs are tended in a positive, caring way see the unconditional love that they have brought into the world *reflected* in parental interaction. When a child looks into the mirror of her parents' faces, she sees joy, happiness, love, connection. Her parents go out of their way to make direct contact with her whenever possible. Changing a diaper or taking a bath involves verbal, physical, and emotional interaction. Even though this baby isn't speaking yet, the message she is receiving from the world around her mirrors her basic goodness. She is given the foundation for true self-esteem.

We can create an environment—physical, psychological, and emotional—for our child in which she is valued and accepted for *herself*. This environment will reflect core values—openness, happiness, appreciation, loving-kindness, and support. We can regard our homes as sacred places that encourage companionship, communication, curiosity, and humor. We can make a generous, spacious psychological atmosphere in which we are committed not only to mirror our children's openness and delight back to them, but also to engage them, to respect them, and to listen to them with our hearts.

We can accept our children as teachers, for they reflect us back to ourselves. Although it is of benefit to know the basic developmental tasks of each age range so that we can support our children in their changing needs, openness to our children is more helpful than all the books we could ever read on child development. When we listen to our children with our hearts, we hear them, we resonate with them, and we are able to respond in a way that lets them know they are loved.

Our children teach us patience. In entering their world, we slow down. Cutting through our mental and physical speed is an opportunity to cultivate inner awareness.

Sometimes listening to silence is as helpful as listening to words. I know a couple whose initiation into birth was as parents of a colicky baby. All their preconceptions of a delightful and peaceful beginning with the baby were shattered by Jessica's miserable screams, which often continued for hours at a time. When the baby blossomed into a gurgling, happy six-month-old, I asked how they had managed to get through the months of colic. They reported that after much anxiety and frustration at their futile efforts to relieve her pain, they learned to listen to the silence around their baby's cries. In effect, they learned to listen to the space between heartbeats.

Two ordinary facts about life on earth that we can point out to our children are impermanence and the relationship between cause and effect. We can teach them about impermanence in positive ways, such as celebrating the changing seasons. We can encourage them to be curious about the twin miracles of birth and death. When they break something, drop their cookie, spill their milk, or have their shoes stolen at the gym, we can model empathy, support, and lightheartedness. We can react fluidly. Some parents I know practice saying, "Well, that's impermanence!" at moments like these.

We can also show our children the relationship between cause and effect. This moves them toward self-responsibility, which grows into empowerment. Almost any event can be used in this regard. It's a matter of tuning in to the many precious opportunities to teach. For example, if the dog chews a favorite toy—or even the homework—we don't have to respond in a castigating way such as, "How many times have I told you not to do your homework on the floor?" Instead, we can subtly point out cause and effect: "How do you think the dog got your homework?"

It is quite likely that our own story lines, the story lines of our own parents, and the filter through which we see the world are going to become entangled in our parenting. Most of us need to reparent ourselves before we can more consistently remain in soul awareness. We need to give ourselves unconditional love and break the cycle experienced by so many families of passing only conditional love to the next generation.

Thus, in inviting children to the path of heart, one of the most generous gifts we can give is to recognize our own projections. Through continual practice of core values, we can make space in which the child can be truly himself—not who we want him to be, or who we think he should be. We can use the words "should" and "must" only to keep him from danger.

We can allow our children to find the balance that comes from within. We can exert positive control—helping him learn to listen with his heart, encouraging her to follow her passions, recognizing our own projections, quieting the voices of our *own* parents in our minds. Children are what they are—essence. We do not need to add what we think they *should be* on top of that.

One day Charlie taught me a very powerful lesson about love. He said out of the blue, "I have to marry Aurora" (his classmate). I said, "Why do you have to marry Aurora?" I couldn't tell where he was coming from. Then he said, "They celebrate the Shabbat, just like we do."

And then I saw his pain: a seven-year-old having to think that he has to marry someone who celebrates the same tradition. I told him from the bottom of my heart, "Charlie, you're a free being. You don't have to do that." I decided to relieve any beliefs he was having about what he "must" do.

He hugged me and thanked me, and I have never heard gratitude coming from such a deep place. Then we meditated for a while. Charlie loves to meditate. When we had finished, he gave me a look and made a particular gesture that involves making a three-dimensional circle with one hand, ending with the palm up, as if he were offering something. There's only one other person I've seen do that: the Dalai Lama.

Happiness during the earlier stages of life creates a valuable passport, a frame of reference for later life, because all experiences are matched to this early subjective learning. The connection between parent and child is profoundly deep. If we model an attitude of unconditional love, joy, and happiness, our children will have an ever-increasing positive attitude and the promise of peace and security for life.

Work and Vocation

When we are fulfilled in our personal lives, we have a very basic desire to make a difference in this world, to contribute something unique. Inner fulfillment and outer contribution are interrelated. To the degree that we cultivate one, the other can be more fully realized.

As we become increasingly aware of who we truly are, as we expand our limited ego-awareness toward essence, we enter into a deeper awareness of our true purpose in this world. Becoming attuned to this purpose, we move into harmony with its natural unfolding.

There is an old adage that says, "God has a destiny for each of us, and of course he has one for you." Each of us has a unique and significant gift. This gift is our true purpose in life; it can involve many complex abilities, or it can be something quite one-pointed like parenthood. In every case, however, it will involve the truth of our innermost selves as essence—a realization of our original blueprint.

As a result, it will be something that we love doing,

something that we are passionate about and that we cannot help but commit ourselves to. Passion and commitment are signs that we are bringing our truth into the world. We are in flow with our lives, allowing the river of life to direct us rather than struggling to direct it by trying to swim upstream.

Everything can be done from the consciousness of inner truth. This extension of the spiritual self (as in all traditions) is also the recognition of the presence of others, which translates itself into compassion, love, and service-oriented action, not more self-gratification.

Buddhism is a good example. One day I asked the Dalai Lama what happens after one reaches buddhahood and he cried, saying that then one practices being a bodhisattva (one who vows to help all beings attain enlightenment). Someone in the audience said, "But isn't that the way to become a buddha?" The Dalai Lama smiled and added, "Becoming a buddha is the aim of all bodhisattvas, so that when they are a buddha, they can be a real servant."

When we wake up to eternity, we are no longer trying to reach it. Therefore we can dedicate energy to the projects in the small story and they become easier to fulfill. Survival is not dependent on them, enlightenment is not dependent on them, happiness is not dependent on them; but they are still valuable. Being valuable means they connect with core values.

Every day, the heart is left behind in jobs, expectations, relationships with self and others. We close our hearts, disconnecting ourselves from the true "blood flow" of love. Then we suffer the consequences of stress, pain, and disconnection.

Even if we have justifiable and legitimate reasons to close down, it is not advisable. Because it happens on so many occasions, we need to remember how to transmute negative emotions into positive ones. In that way we can continue to use everything that comes our way for the sake of our life-force commitment.

What do I mean by this? Do what you love, do what your heart will enjoy; do it with enthusiasm, with interest, or don't do it at all. But how can we do that when we have to hold a job? Many of us blame our jobs for uneasiness, ill health, unsatisfying relationships, and deviations from original intent, instead of taking inner responsibility for our lack of balance.

When our current employment and soul purpose don't match, we can bring them into alignment. We do this by becoming aware of the opportunities for mindfulness and awareness in our job. We either make them match by changing our attitude, or move on to something else. A Buddhist slogan says, "Change your attitude and relax as it is." If we relax where we are and align ourselves with essence, we can do whatever we are doing and still benefit others.

If we take a deep breath, "time out" our thought process, and ask the inner voice of the heart, the voice of the core values, "What am I here to do?" we come up with intuitive answers. If we then empower ourselves with the intention of organizing consciousness into this voice, we do what is in alignment.

I remember a woman who took a workshop with me a long time ago. She was forty-plus years old, divorced, and had three children. She hadn't begun any other romantic relationships since her divorce. She was shy and fed up with being a secretary. That's when she came to my seminar. After working with her I received a letter telling me how much she appreciated what I had taught her. She also said that she used to get frustrated by her typewriter, and now she had learned to love her typewriter. "I never thought I could love my typewriter!" She realized that being a secretary could be a spiritual exercise.

Everyone has a vocation. If you hypnotize a person who is unhappy with what he is doing, you will discover that at some point in his life he did have a vision. He had a mission and something may have happened to interrupt it. Maybe his parents said "Get real" or "Find something that's suited for you." He was encouraged to be practical or realistic. So he studied how to make it in the world, and ultimately became successful, but he is still unhappy because he didn't listen to his heart.

I knew a doctor who was such a good pianist when he was a child that he won an international contest. His mother, who was also a pianist, thought that music wouldn't be enough for her child, so she forced him into intellectual activities that he really had no interest in. So he studied and became a psychologist.

This man was never interested in people; he was interested in playing music for people. He had a very unhappy life and couldn't get himself to commit deeply to anything. But there was one thing that he could do well: play the piano. At a certain point in his life he became sick. He came and spoke with me, and I saw that behind the physiological situation there was something else. I saw this when he told me he liked giving talks, except he didn't know what to do with his hands.

We did an exercise. If his hands could talk, what would they say? He began moving his hands as if playing the piano, and then his hands said to him that what they were made for was to play the piano. There was a piano in my house, and he sat down to play. He realized he had suppressed his own vocation for fifty years.

I recommended that he simply play more. When we have a job in life that is not our inner vocation, we are not condemned to a life of unhappiness. The way to realizing inner happiness is still open to us. On the other hand we might be the best pianist, but if there's no love it won't make any difference.

No matter what we do, whether or not we feel aligned with our inner vocation, work provides an opportunity to tune in to the higher frequencies of core values and to be of service to others. No matter how menial our work, we have the chance to convey warmth, generosity, patience, and love in all our dealings.

Once we know that thoughts and feelings are frequencies of energy, it makes sense to know which frequencies add to our personal power. We can choose our own frequencies; we can take responsibility for ourselves and stop being victims. We have a choice in how to react in certain circumstances. If we have more power in our hearts to manage our reactions, we have better responses. We can achieve balance and fulfillment in the midst of chaos because we know exactly where our sacred territory is. It's *here*, in the present moment; that's the only place it is.

In the 1987 stock market crash, people realized that money doesn't buy peace, happiness, and security. In the third dimension money can create a feeling of security, in one frequency. But it is a false sense of security because it relates to only one nafs. We can build a complete security band of frequency within ourselves through the self-empowerment that comes from essence. And then we can cultivate true practice—which is to come from the stability of essential identity in any situation.

INNER WORK AT WORK

The challenges of the third dimension offer the chance to implement a stronger power than our habitual thoughts and feelings. This hidden power of the heart operates at a higher range of frequency than the mind.

When we feel resentment toward someone, or when we recognize disdain or the desire for revenge, we can consciously remember all the good that we know of that person. We can remember good times we had in his company before being hurt by him. We can dwell on his good qualities. If we manage to remember a joke that he told or something funny that we enjoyed together, the miracle is achieved. We can summon the positive memory as many times as necessary in transmuting our resentment.

This involves turning the other cheek. It involves loving our enemies, blessing those who curse us, doing well to those who detest us, and praying for those who persecute us. If we practice this genuinely, strange things might happen. First we will feel liberated, and then a mountain of small inconveniences and obstacles might well begin to disappear as if by enchantment. We might then begin to notice that we are loved by all the world, even by people who didn't wish us well before.

Another way to deal with problems at work is to accept the situation and make it bigger. Loving broadens awareness. It is the ground of true understanding. This is problem-solving from the path of heart.

First, surrender to heaven and earth, acknowledging the workplace as sacred space. Feel gratitude and appreciation for your situation. Then mentally define the problem and activate essential loving identity by imagining yourself to be a warm, pulsating, golden light. Taking a deep breath, inhale the energy of whatever problem you are trying to solve. Then, breathing out golden light-rays of love toward your co-workers, see their essential identity as well. By continuing to transfer loving energy in this way, you can activate a power circuit of connectedness. Then, as solutions arise, consider those that are in alignment with the universal frequency of the human family. If your co-workers are interested, practice decision-making by consensus, undertaking no solution to which even one person has a serious objection.

Sometimes through our work we may feel that we are forcing ourselves unhappily to fulfill the small-story agenda. When we feel inauthentic with someone as a soul but helpless to shift the energy to a more genuine level, we become frustrated. In instances that involve others, it is best to let them know how we are feeling. Usually they are feeling inauthentic also, and would welcome the opportunity to interact on a more genuine level. Instead of making the statement "*You* need this," we can say "*I* need this." Focusing on our own reality will provoke fewer defensive feelings in the other person.

We can let these instances be stepping-stones to a greater grace. We can take some time for ourselves, be in silence, re-center, meditate, pray, make a decision, and from this perspective assume the position of authenticity. The point is to break whatever we are doing with the intention of re-centering, re-grouping our soul purpose for five minutes.

In Venezuela I knew a businessman who was not in touch with his essential identity. He was blocked not only emotionally but also physically. He'd had a coronary bypass at age forty-two. I was having lunch with him at a very elegant club. I was feeling awkward. I didn't know how to connect with him. I felt uncomfortable. So I went to the bathroom, and while I was there I thought of the Pope and his humanness—the common denominator.

I went back to the table and said to the businessman, "Were you born in a very poor family?" He broke wide open. "Yes, my father left my mother when we were little and my mother raised seven kids. Sometimes we didn't have soup to eat or anything. But now I'm a powerful businessman. I have my own airplane."

I said to him, "When will you have enough to prove yourself; when you destroy your whole system? Because you still haven't gotten it. You've made it, but what's next in life? Have you made it inwardly?"

I invited him to a workshop, but he never came. In fact, he died three years later in Texas. He worked himself to death. He left a fortune. So what? Did he have core values? No. He was still trying to compensate for his mother not having enough soup for seven children.

We must recognize when we are motivated to compensate for something that we feel is lacking—physical, mental, or emotional. This requires intense inner exertion. Did we grow up thinking that we had to please others to be loved? Then is our work motivated by the desire to please? Did we feel that other people were always ahead of us somehow? Then we might feel that we have to prove ourselves intellectually, even if it's by designing nuclear weapons! Did we feel responsible for our parents' shortcomings? Our subconscious motivation at work might be to always try to make things better for others, while ignoring our own needs. Huge successes have been made by riding the energy of psychological compensation. But true success lies in inner realization.

There is no greater success than being genuinely and honestly oneself, inside and outside. Whatever we do to make money, if we align it with the path of heart, we can use our occupation or vocation to reflect to others the healing energy of the divine. This is especially true with those who have decided to make their living by healing and helping others: doctors, nurses, practitioners of alternative medicine, social workers, volunteers, and so on. For them, using divine energy in their jobs is essential.

Between Healer and Patient

It is the function of the human being we call doctor to be present in the experience of total health. Health is a state of physical, psychic, social, spiritual, and ecological well-being.

When we talk about spiritual well-being, we are not speaking of religion but rather of contact with the center of our forces, and thereby contact with divine energy. If health has so many facets, then we must understand that the altered states of health that we call illness also have many facets. Many times as doctors we forget this and concentrate our education solely on "curing" a particular illness. But medicine has a purpose in a much larger context, because the state of health requires constant interaction.

To aid in the maintenance of health, the greatest offerings that a doctor can make are love, communication, contact, and interaction. These gifts are the core values that a genuine doctor must bring to the relationship with his patient. In other words, first a physician must heal himself.

Self-love is the way to attain mastery in healing. If we are physicians, it is how we genuinely tend to the sick. If we ourselves are sick, it is how we heal. Even—and especially—illness can be an initiation into the higher realms of awareness.

For example, I once had a patient with colon cancer. He had already had the cancerous part of his intestine surgically removed at a prestigious New York hospital, and he had undergone several courses of radiation therapy to kill any cancer cells that might have escaped the knife. In spite of this treatment, new precancerous polyps were already emerging on the healthy part of his colon. Even alternative therapies such as Chinese herbs and therapeutic touch were having no effect on the cancer.

When he could finally take the pain no more, he cried out, "I can't delay this any longer!" He meant that the time had come to ask for divine assistance, despite the fact that he was an atheist.

At that moment a veil of light appeared to him. He saw his entire life flash before his eyes. In his heart he knew he was going to die. So he surrendered. At that moment he transcended his mortal, physical self and for the first time in his life saw his essential self. He saw the part of him that would live forever in spite of the death of his physical body. However, his death was not imminent.

This incident changed my patient. The cancer beat a hasty retreat. Five years later, he is thriving.

What happened? What was the power hidden within my patient, and what caused it to come out when it did? When he surrendered to his fate, he contacted the healing power of his essential identity. He discovered that real healing is rooted in a higher level of awareness.

As a healer, I have discovered that giving a patient choices, or letting anyone know they have alternatives, can be a powerful healing all by itself. Healthy people are constantly growing, changing, and evolving. To every person who comes to me, I wish peace. If they are at peace with themselves, they begin to share the very nature of their being. I hold the space, recognize the other as a spiritual being, and encourage a heart-to-heart relationship. When we listen from the heart, the quality of our communication changes so that we can truly hear each other, and the healing dance begins.

When we have this kind of communication, we can work together to find therapeutic actions to confront the sources of illness rather than simply alleviate the symptoms.

Today, unfortunately, there are a myriad of specialists who treat symptoms and measure success by the number of patients they can see in a day, without regard to the quality of these contacts. They should not act as robots and treat patients as if on an assembly line. The answer is a much older and broader approach.

We must return to a re-evaluation of our basic educational process as healers and place more emphasis on self-development and self-awareness. Realizing the *spirit* of the healing arts enables both doctor and patient to better understand and improve the interaction needed to improve health, and in doing so improve the quality of life itself. We can help the patient focus on her strengths—areas in which she is healthy and flowing—rather than simply treating her as a sick person. We can encourage core values by modeling them ourselves. This is how the healing pyramid evolves.

As patients choosing a healer, we can ask ourselves the following questions:

Does this person seem to know who he is as a human being?

Is she involved in inner work or a spiritual practice of any kind?

Does he seem to approach healing as a "job" or a "vocation"?

Does she seem to place herself above me in any way?

Is he interested in my total experience, or only my symptoms?

Do I feel relaxed at appointments?

Does this person keep me waiting?

Is she curious about my belief structure?

Does he treat my diagnosis as an absolute label, or as a workable condition?

Does she approach me as a sick person or as a spiritual being?

When both healer and patient are responsible, empowered, and committed to the values of the heart, the healing relationship becomes a sacred space in which essence comes to the fore. By activating our connection with divine energy, we can use what has manifested as illness as an external reference point from which a greater awareness and more genuine well-being can emerge.

Death as Initiation

The universe has many levels of being and consciousness. Although we do not perceive all dimensions, they co-exist with those to which we have opened. Spirit exists at different frequencies of vibration, much like the waves in electromagnetic fields. Thus, the physical body is an expression of a certain frequency. When it dissolves, our essence remains but its vibrations are no longer readily perceivable by the senses of those we leave behind.

Death, like conception and birth, is one of the most mysterious of initiations. The elements that have come together to make up the physical body separate, and the life force leaves. We journey through other vibratory levels and through *bardos* (a Tibetan word meaning "in-between states") after leaving our bodies behind.

In these different frequencies we awaken to experiences that may represent unfinished business from our physical manifestation. We get in touch with karmic memories. Then we re-emerge, reincarnate, preferably in a higher level of awareness. Death is not a final state but a transformation of consciousness.

The best preparation for death is to live from essence. Knowing that our embodied life in the third dimension is also a kind of bardo—the space between physical birth and physical death—is a wholesome attitude. His Holiness the Dalai Lama stops seven times a day to meditate on dying and crossing the bardo. One day I was sitting in the living room in Dharamsala when he came back from his prayers. I looked at him, and he said, "That was the fifth time today." He's been doing it for fifty years. Then he said, "Well, when I die, finally I'll see if it worked!"

Practicing inner awareness is not a guarantee that we'll get a medal when we die. In practice we are training our mind to become flexible, like bamboo, so that it can dance and move when the higher winds call for it. We're so busy that we don't usually even think about life being an opportunity to practice for death. But birth and death occur with each new moment.

Even experiencing the death of a loved one can be a major initiation into previously unknown dimensions. When the bonds between us are strong, our connection is palpable beyond our physical bodies. For example, when my mother's cancer had progressed and she had gone through chemotherapy, I was traveling in Europe when I felt a psychic call. I was at the Vatican Museums one Sunday morning in late October 1985 when Carolina and I went back to her aunt's house, where we were staying. I called Chile. My mother sounded weak but told me that she was feeling better than she had felt for the previous few days. Over long distance I asked her, "What is that sound?" "Oh nothing," she said, "just oxygen."

This was enough for me to end the conversation, pack a bag, and fly twenty-seven hours from Rome to Buenos Aires to Santiago. I knew my mother was dying, and I wanted to be close to her. I arrived exhausted, bought flowers, and went to her home. For seven days and seven nights I accompanied her in the cyclical changes that a human being close to death seems to go through.

I went from irrational hope to grief to using alternative techniques of healing. I went through all the emotions. On the last night, my mother described herself as lying in a cathedral and described the face of someone who was going to take her body away. She died the next morning very early while I was holding her hand, as I had promised many years before.

I sat with the body in state, listening to a piece by Kobialka, "Fragments of a Dream," praying and blessing her. I felt like a high priest accompanying her to the other side. As people were coming into the room, they were astonished at how full of light, how young, how beautiful she looked. The grimaced pain of the cancer had lifted and she was becoming a body of light before our eyes. When the funeral directors came to take her body, I was shocked to see that the face of one of the men was exactly as she had described it the night before.

I felt at one with her in my consciousness. But I also felt orphaned; the veil between life and death had been torn, and an aspect of my own child—not the "inner child," but the son of my mother—had become orphaned. I was initiated into another dimension of life. I knew that the angel of death had taken her generation and that in a way I was next.

A few days after my mother's funeral I went to Europe specifically to meet with the psychologist Carl Rogers and the former President of Costa Rica Dr. Rodrigo Carazo and other dignitaries to be part of a peace conference on the Central American conflict. It was late 1985 and that conflict was intense.

I felt that I postponed my grief then to be of service, but after the mediation was over, Carolina and I flew back to South America for my father's eightieth birthday. Then I began my year of grieving.

In the Jewish Kabbalistic tradition we sit seven days of mourning, since it is taught that the sensory-motor aspect of the expression of the soul separates after one week. It is like having a going-away ceremony for the dead. The feeling spirit departs after thirty days, and after one year the individual consciousness departs. I definitely felt the lifting after one year. Throughout this whole period, I communicated with my mother inwardly.

I used my sadness, grief, tears, and longing as ways to communicate. When my grief subsided, I asked her questions. Our dialogue taught me about intention and manifestation. It definitely served as an initiation into the power to be in the flow and continually bring spirit into matter.

About three years later my father was in the hospital with kidney problems. I was advised by my medical colleagues to do nothing. Kidney dialysis was, they said, expensive, difficult, and complicated. They gave me all kinds of stupid reasons not to do it.

Carolina was newly pregnant with Alexandra. My father was dying. I decided to find out what was true for us. One night at 3:00 A.M. I was at the hospital. Dad and I were weeping, saying goodbye, completing all unfinished business. I said, "If you see Mom on the other side, say hello."

Once this farewell had happened, I felt a great inner strength. The room seemed full of light. So I said very energetically, "I command you to get well in the name of the Supreme Light. Please, if it is for the highest good, stay amongst us because I love you and need to be in your presence."

He looked at me and said, "Didn't we say goodbye? Leave me alone."

I left the room. At eight o'clock in the morning I returned. The bed was stripped and there was no one in the silent room, not even a nurse. I thought, "God almighty, he is dead!"

But then the bathroom door opened and my father appeared. He smiled and said, "I'm shaving. If you want me around, I'd better look decent."

I embraced him with deep love and said, "I don't mean to force you, but what would you do if the roles were reversed?"

He answered, "Anything to keep you alive."

I said, "I will also."

After twelve successful dialysis treatments, we celebrated his eighty-third birthday with violins in the garden. During this time we had a connection of deep love. He told me that he would take our long embrace with him to the other side, and also that he had not felt this quality of love since he was very young and free.

Eight months after his hospitalization, his condition deteriorated. It was as if the angels of life were bringing in Alexandra, who was due to be born in a month, as the angels of death were taking my father away. He said, "If there is something on the other side, I'll let you know."

I looked and saw in my father the divine union. All the aspects of the divine were in his face. I knew we were one.

On the afternoon of his passing I fell asleep at my father's side holding his arm. I dreamed that I was being propelled through a tunnel of light. Approaching a bend in the tunnel, I was awakened by the nurse. She asked me to leave the room while she took his temperature. I left the room, walked down the corridor, and was paged.

He had waited for me to leave the room to take that turn in the tunnel of light. He died while I was outside.

I practiced all the necessary spiritual rituals for him. Forty days later my deep grief was alleviated by the waterbirth of Alexandra. As I said in an earlier chapter, it was an extremely powerful birth initiation.

A few weeks after my daughter was born I had a curious experience. Someone led me to a pastry shop. I walked in and asked for a chocolate rum ball. The woman behind the counter said, "Nonsense. You are here because you want to know about your dad's destiny."

I was shocked. We went into the back room, and she went into a trance. Then she spoke in my father's voice. "Dear son, have no tears because where I am is more splendid than I ever dreamed possible. Intelligence, golden light, and love surround me—more than I could ever imagine on earth. Follow your path because it is correct, and we will meet again some time. Don't grieve, for there is nothing to be sad about. I love you."

What a completion. What an initiation.

❖ EXERCISE ❖
FULL ENERGY EXCHANGE

This is an exercise you can do whenever you feel that you or someone else is suffering. You can do it when your child's feelings are hurt and he is crying; you can do it when someone you know is ill; you can do it when you've watched upsetting news on television; you can do it when you see an accident or pass a hospital.

First, imagine the power of heaven and earth and surrender totally to it. Take a deep breath. Imagine that as you inhale the divine energy around you, you are as spacious and empty as it seems to be. Now flash awareness of yourself as essence—a nonsolid entity.

Visualize yourself or whoever it is that is suffering. See them standing in front of you in all their pain. This can be your parent, your child, your co-worker, your spouse— anyone. Imagine their suffering with all your heart. Try to imagine its quality, and try to imagine exactly how they are feeling.

Now with a deep breath take all their suffering into your being. Imagine their pain as deep black, unbearably hot, and claustrophobic. When doing this practice, it is important to visualize your whole body taking in the darkness of pain. Visualize the darkness and heaviness of pain entering through every one of your pores.

Hold their pain in your heart and pray that you can take on all of their pain.

Now, as you exhale, visualize streams of rainbow light traveling out through every pore of your being. Imagine the person in front of you absorbing all this luminous energy. With your breath, send your most sincere and genuine wish that their suffering might be relieved.

Again, take in all their suffering as hot, heavy, and dark energy. On the outbreath, send out rainbow light. Imagine with each of your inbreaths and outbreaths that their burden is becoming lighter.

When you stabilize your heart-energy in this practice, you can make it bigger. Now you can imagine all the people in the world who are feeling the way this person is feeling, standing in front of you. You can take on all the pain of all the people in all the world who are feeling the way this hurt soul feels right now. You can send out to them ocean waves of luminous rainbow light in exchange for their pain.

When you have done this practice for several minutes or longer, you can first dissolve the visualization in front of you into rainbow light. Then you can dissolve yourself into rainbow light. Then you can rest in the nature of infinite essence.

CHAPTER TWELVE

❖

Moving Toward the Now Age

To be alive is to be in a state of progress, a singular experience unique to each of us. Every one of us is a unique gem of incomparable worth to ourselves, not by what we accomplish or what we obtain but rather by the way in which we learn to live and by the discovery of who we essentially are.

To learn to live is to learn to know ourselves and to create a space in which we can inspire ourselves to continue to grow and evolve. In writing this book, I have tried to describe how we can create that space.

As we create our own sacred space, we can continue to enlarge it. We've seen how it can include our lover, our children, our co-workers. We can make it even bigger than that. When we connect with the divine energy at the top of the healing pyramid, we can enlarge our sense of space to include everyone on earth and in every other dimension of existence.

As we realize our true self, the power of love and the present moment come together. When we are One we can truly surrender to God, transcending "I am" to "It is."

That is magic, where healing happens. It evolves from our genuine relationship with self, others, and the divine energy available to all of us in every moment.

God in Me, God in You

Einstein discovered that everything is energy, and then quantum physics added that nothing is separate. Quantum reality is different from the mechanics of Newtonian reality. It has shown us that everything in the universe is connected in an interdependent dance, and that there is no solidity at all—just waves and energy patterns from the microscopic to the macroscopic level.

In taking responsibility and empowering ourselves at the second level of the healing pyramid, we buy ourselves a ticket to this dance. Of course, we're already at the dance, but we've been "sitting it out." As we begin to free ourselves from the limitations of temporary identities, we can join the dance. We can participate in the dance of connection and be the protagonist of our lives in the big story of evolution.

This dance doesn't stop. The more we dance, the more open our hearts become, and we tune in to energy frequencies at the next level of the pyramid—core values such as love, caring, forgiveness, gratitude, and compassion—that keep the dance going.

At the top of the healing pyramid we connect directly with the higher power of divine healing energy. There's no longer any "me"; there's just the dance. And in the dance we find love and the remembrance of our own divinity.

The vibratory frequency of divine energy is always available to us, whether or not we directly connect with it. But when we live in it consciously from essence, we are freed from never-ending recovery and cleansing, working it out, problem solving, and self-limiting fears and phobias. With this elevated viewpoint and attitude, we can use the divine energy within our bodies without having to be obsessed with survival. Then we have a surplus of never-ending energy that we can dedicate to serving others. We tap into our own cornucopia, the infinite force of potential and abundance.

The wisdom and compassion available at this level take us beyond all fixed ideas. Our open heart and our commitment to being awake have become habitual. We experience a smooth, streamlined efficiency. From this perspective, events that once might have seemed stressful now are seen as untransformed opportunities for love and empowerment. So we bring heaven to earth.

In this book I have tried to be helpful in describing how we might open ourselves in such a way. However, I would like to point out that enlightenment, unconditional joy, and unconditional love are not something we acquire as our hearts open. We are, at all times, blessed with divinity. It is our life purpose to wake up to that. Many years ago, when I first met the late Willis Harman, past president of the Institute of Noetic Sciences—then a regent of the University of California—we talked only of science. The next morning he phoned me and said, "Carlos, isn't it time that we come out of the closet and truly communicate? Aren't we really agents of the holy spirit?" I was very deeply moved.

Yes, we need to come out of the closet with our enlightenment, our experience of essence. It is something that we are, rather than something that we have. We often become blasé after hearing things like I'm saying. The head says, "I've already heard that." But the reason our open hearts beat is to take us into the fifth-dimensional aspect of this soul, which is union or *yehida* ("uniqueness") in Kabbalistic terms, or *yakina* ("certainty") in Sufi terms.

We can be "I am"—the container for my body, my mind, my spirit, and this bliss-body of unconditional joy, which Buddhists call *mahasukha* and Sufis and Kabbalists call *jaya*—while we're given the grace to be here. And then the healing path truly opens and worlds of alignment take place.

We speak of gratitude. For what? For life. For the grace of being here. For joy as pure joy. I work with people who've been heads of state, and they say, "If I'd known then what life is all about, I would've acted differently, but I got trapped with the temptation of power, trapped in the temptation of control." As we have seen, we are all subject to multiple traps. But we are all also subject to the ability to open our hearts and go beyond the traps.

My model of the healing pyramid is really only that—a model. It is a helpful way of looking at the transition from consensus reality to unity consciousness.

No matter what level of the pyramid we're focusing on, divine energy comes through directly. God doesn't talk about dimensions. The energy of the universe is right here from all interdimensional viewpoints. And the dimensions exist simultaneously. We can access the divine field from anywhere, no matter who we are: a peasant, a scientist, a homemaker. It's everywhere, and it's immediately available in the present moment. Thus, I can access it without having to cross dimensions. I can be in God while I'm ironing shirts. God is multidimensional and simultaneous.

Love, Wisdom, and Action

There is a level of intelligence that is the intelligence of God. This comes through channels that we call human beings; when these channels of perception are open, we manifest ourselves in love, wisdom, and action. This intelligence involves the capacity to open ourselves and flow with the situation. We can balance these three areas in order to awaken the consciousness of service.

LOVE

If we declare peace with ourselves, we learn to love ourselves and then to love others. When we fondly love the person next to us, we can expand that circle to include all humanity. The result of this peace is love, and the result of this love is happiness.

Each of us is a dynamic association of cells forming an organism called a human being, man or woman. To imagine and to resemble the visualization of the creator, these units are an expression of the integration of all their ideas, beliefs, and actions. The uniting force of the molecules of each of these beings, and of each of these pairs of beings (or groups of beings, or communities, nations, and cultures), is love.

Pierre Teilhard de Chardin said, "The day will come when, after harnessing the winds, the tides, and gravitation, we shall harness for God the energies of love. And on that day, for the second time in the history of the world, man will have discovered fire." That day is upon us, and I call it the Now Age.

To love is to recognize divine energy in ourselves and in others. To see God in both is the real encounter with love.

Love is most important of all. It is the golden door to paradise. We can pray for understanding of love and meditate upon it daily. We can exile any fear and substitute faith in its place. Indeed, the core value of faith lights our way on the path of heart.

There is no difficulty that cannot be conquered with sufficient love, no chasm so treacherous that it cannot be crossed with sufficient love. There is no wall that a sufficient amount of love cannot bring down. There is no sin that a sufficient amount of love cannot redeem.

It doesn't matter how entrenched is the error, nor how desperate the phenomenon, nor how great the mistake, nor how entangled the involvement: if we can love sufficiently, we will be the most powerful and happiest beings on earth. That is optimum physiology.

WISDOM

The ground of true wisdom is knowing that we are eternal and also that we will die. When we balance this knowledge with love and action, we practice in the presence of God.

When we practice in the presence of God, we are surrendering to heaven and earth. This is an enormous space in which we are willing to dance with no reference point at all. Going beyond our limiting beliefs takes us into an incredibly rich realm of holographic awareness. Here we have the opportunity to radiate core values. We do not *have* them; we vibrate at their higher frequencies. We radiate the vibrations of gratitude, generosity, discipline, patience, love, compassion, gentleness, precision, forgiveness, exertion, and curiosity. We are energy energized by God.

Wisdom is our guide, and it manifests in the world of

external phenomena. We understand now that what seems to be outside ourselves reflects our inner state, which is one of fluidity, vitality, and change. And we understand that the creation around us is also energy. It is a vivid expression of sound, light, movement, vibration, color, and pattern. Through wisdom we communicate with this energy very directly, without concept, because through the openness of our being the world speaks to us.

And we answer. Our wisdom expresses itself in words, in silence, and in action.

The Wisdom of Speech

Each word that we pronounce is a declaration that is manifested in the world around us. The word is the thought spoken.

To become aware of the power of our words, for one whole day we should notice what we say. Let's remember it all. We may find ourselves making lower-frequency remarks such as "Business is horrible." "Things are going very badly." "It's too good to be true." "I can't take it anymore." "Traffic is impossible." "I can't eat that; it'll make me sick."

We shouldn't be surprised to see that what we say often comes to pass. However, alignment with higher frequencies presents the opportunity to use words as gateways to higher frequencies. For example, "It will be all right." "I know I can do it." "I trust this situation." "Let's be cheerful." "What delicious food!"—these remarks open us and those around us to the incredible abundance and beauty of the sacred world.

Whatever we say comes back to us. If we are kind and understanding toward someone, then we receive kindness and understanding. That is how situations evolve in a harmonious way. We have the power to perform miracles through our speech.

In my encounters with many sacred traditions, I have learned the importance of considering the spiritual well-being of all. It is important to seek illumination for all conscious beings and not only for ourselves. This is the unity of experience in which healing occurs, and it reinforces our own power to heal ourselves and others. When we revert to former habitual patterns of speech—for example, criticism or complaint—for the good of all we can recognize what is happening and leave those words unspoken. Benediction is good speech; malediction is a curse.

When we are with other people, we can clearly notice their language. When we hear negative conversations, we can remain silent. We can protect our inner awareness and affirm the goodness of beings by saying to ourselves, "I don't accept that as true for me, nor for them." We don't have to try to change what others say. Just one act of conscious awareness has the power to automatically alter the emotional frequency of a group interaction. We needn't proselytize. From wisdom and love, we can act in alignment with higher truth. In many cases, that is the most powerful way to teach others.

Silence

Silent practice helps us create sacred space. We create sacred space in our minds and hearts through prayer, meditation, and deep relaxation. We create this space in our homes by establishing silent times during which we are not interrupted by the telephone, television, radio, the noise of electrical appliances, and so on. With our families we can celebrate a time of silence before meals, in which we all withdraw to pray, meditate, or simply *be*—quietly. In these centered silent spaces we practice patience, tolerance, acceptance, gratitude. Silent space creates a balance between inner and outer life.

We can periodically review our practice of silence by asking ourselves questions like these:

Did I create an environment to facilitate silence today?

When ego reactions arose, did I take time to re-center within the silence of the soul?

Did I conserve energy through the silence of speech?

How does silence help me to focus on my purpose?

How and when was I silent?

What is silence? How is it related to the recognition of my intent of my life purpose?

How have I benefited myself and others through silence?

At what other times might I practice it?

Action

True action is interaction with the present moment. Surrendering to heaven and to earth, we engage ourselves totally with the task at hand. Even something seemingly mundane like cleaning house can be a complete expression of the openness of our hearts. We can appreciate each object we clean, and appreciate the space around the objects. In feeling the objects, we are touching the earth; in feeling the space, we are acknowledging the lightness, peace, and divine energy that are

everywhere. Being open to our world in this way culti-
vates a state of ongoing meditation.

When we are truly present in our actions, there is no
actor, only action. It is not "me" washing dishes; it is
dishes washing. It is not "me" writing book; it is book
writing. It is not "me" cooking food; it is food cooking. It
is not "me" being doctor; it is doctor being.

Connecting totally with our activity infuses it with a
drop of sweetness that comes from feeling appreciation
for our life. It is to live in gratitude for the mystery that we
did not create, but in which we are creating. Enlightened
activity involves offering ourselves as a conduit for divine
energy and circulating that energy into everything we
touch, whether it is a baby, a dying person, a pencil, or a
teapot. It involves honoring the sacred in the ordinary,
and at the same time honoring the ordinary in the sacred.
This is healing activity.

Healing activity takes an infinite number of forms. For
example, the Tibetan yogi Milarepa simply sits on a
mountain and vibrates. He isn't concerned with how
many people he's affecting or serving. When we reach
that big-story perspective, it doesn't matter whether we
help one person or one billion people. It depends on
what type of person we are. If we're more introverted, we
may affect only one or two people once we are enlightened. If we are extroverted, we may strive to reach more
people. In the Native American tradition it is believed that
we can change the world with four people: one to go
north, one to go south, one to go east, and one to go
west.

Healing Community

INVITING THE ELDERS AND EXPANDING OUR CIRCLE

Every sacred tradition makes it very clear that healing ourselves means healing our communities. No matter where we live, the earth is the sacred space in which our community evolves. Spiritual community is not just a third-dimensional community. At the physical level, it's the people who are physically present. But our community also includes angels, archangels, and others—enlightened beings who have chosen not to have physical bodies. Ancestors, friends—they are all protecting us.

When I give a talk, I consciously activate a sacred space by invoking the upper-dimensional members of that family—God, the angels, the archangels, my ancestors. And I honor as sacred the space in which I am giving the talk. And when I'm riding in a bus or a boat, I also create a sacred space. I even do it when I sit down to read the *New York Times* or the *Wall Street Journal.*

I like to supplicate and offer my gratitude and love to this global and transglobal community. This is prayer. We can invite these community members to be present as a way of acknowledging our reconnection, even though they are with us whether we invite them or not. With them we can walk in the company of the forces of light.

When we pray, we can also specifically invite these forces to enter our hearts and clear us of any pain, any sorrow, any disease. And if we can offer our hearts as a landing-pad, they will do it. How do they do it? I really don't know. But we can invite them to help us, pray for them to help us, let them help us, and then say "thank you." And then we can offer any benefit we have gained to all others in our community. This is how we keep divine energy flowing.

I was giving a talk in Miami recently just after hearing of the bloody slaughter of hundreds of Rwandans, and I expressed my compassion for the situation and acknowledged the sadness and anger I had felt about this atrocity. An older white woman who identified herself as a therapist asked me how I could be angry at this incident.

"Hundreds of men, women, and children were just cut to pieces with machetes because they were members of the 'wrong' tribe," I told her in amazement. "How can you not have any feeling around it?"

"Oh," she told me, "I just don't let it enter my field."

I looked around the room. There were quite a few black people in the audience. "You can't help having it enter your field. It happened. It exists in our world. Can you honor the event?"

"I don't know any Rwandans, so I don't get involved," she explained aloofly. "It's only real if I experience it."

I took a deep breath and explained slowly, "Who I am, in essence, is dying in Rwanda—not from a philosophical perspective of empathy, but from the knowingness that in essence there exists an inner connectedness with those people in Africa."

"I practice positive thinking, so I don't care," she said in a defiant tone. She looked around her at all the shocked faces and left the lecture hall.

This characterizes the misinterpretation of a lot of New Age self-indulgence. This form of positive thinking is hollow because it has no real, effective service action in the world. It is selfish and lacks compassion. The ideas of positive thinking are quite valid, but they do more harm than good if we stop at the thinking and don't integrate the thoughts and feelings into our being, our actions, and our prayers.

RETURNING TO THE SACRED
IN SICKNESS AND HEALTH

Medicine in the West has forgotten the nature of the soul. Many people in the health-care field are talking about money—where to spend it, where to save it, how to cut costs. Why? Healing the medical system is not about money. It's about remembering the soul in the art of healing.

Recovery of the sacred in medicine is not an academic concern. To heal our medical system, we must honor the sacredness of the human experience. By imagining that the arts of healing are only human, we fail to honor our mystery. In failing to honor the divine mystery, we fall ill.

God is the ultimate Healer. God uses His instruments and His doctors and His surgeons and His herbs and His stones to make us whole. At the ground level of the pyramid, God's gifts are abundant. At the top of the healing pyramid, divine energy makes itself immediately available to us, if we make ourselves available to it. With this energy we can remember our knives and our medicines and our technologies as sacred tools. We can integrate all the resources at hand into full-spectrum healing.

We need to bring God back into medicine. We need to acknowledge that genuine healing requires being present in full interaction with our patients, and in full interaction with God.

Returning to the sacred is not about fixing, adding, or acquiring. It is about remembering something we have hidden. The inner wholeness of the healer is not about *doing* something, but *being* something. For several hundred years we have focused on the state of the body. In forgetting that we have a body but we are *not* the body, we split our mind, body, and spirit. The split is the illusion that permeates our entire society. Coming from this mechanical viewpoint, we ask the wrong questions; and the answers we receive do not serve us.

Our current medical system is focused on mastery. There is mystery when there is mastery, but we're not engaging the mystery. Medicine needs a balance between the two. We have the first medical system in history that allows only for mastery, but not for mystery. Our mastery in terms of life extension, pharmacology, birthing, and so on is wondrous. We can acknowledge the mystery without diminishing the mastery that we have achieved.

Liberating ourselves as healers is as simple as centering our consciousness in our hearts. All esoteric traditions acknowledge that the path to higher intellect is a corridor that leads from the inner heart to the brain. Liberating ourselves involves beginning to discard what is excessive—shamefulness, blame, guilt, fear, ideas that get in the way. The more we eliminate what is excessive, the more clear is our direct line to divine energy. This is how we can integrate our mastery—which is impressive—with the mystery of divine healing energy.

MOVING TOWARD PEACE

My interest is in contributing to a society of souls. A society of souls will change legislation. A society of souls will change education. A society of souls will not have medical schools like I attended more than a quarter of a century ago where a surgery professor told us, "If you have feelings for your patients, you'll never be a good doctor."

I couldn't relate to this attitude, so I went into psychiatry, where I thought I was dealing with the soul, and they told me, "If you pay so much attention to your patients, you're never going to have enough time."

Health and peace are synonymous in the sense that the spiritual goal of health is wholeness and peace. To be at peace is to participate in the rhythm of being. Nonviolence means not causing harm to ourselves or others. It means revering the dignity of every being.

Being in peace doesn't mean that we melt into superficial love-and-lightness and thereafter have no discrimination in how we use our resources. It means that we are in tune with the rhythm of life through a synergy that is active and passive all in one. The adventure of being is the big story. It does not mean regressing to the openness of babyhood; it means unifying the human and the divine. It does not mean overly cultivating open-mindedness. Peace does not mean maintaining the status quo. It is a flux and a flow toward cosmic harmony.

It is very difficult for people to live without external peace, but it is impossible to live without internal peace.

Every sacred tradition encourages us to move toward peace. Christ suffered for the sake of humankind and showed us the power of transformation through his resurrection. The Buddha unraveled the connection between suffering and desire and showed us how to move beyond both to a sublime inner peace.

We are confronted with the search for truth, which involves the discovery of what it is to be truly free in life. This is an internal freedom by which we can be comfortable in many circumstances, since the place in which it reigns is the infinite within the finite.

Depression is the illness of this century because no one is living to his or her fullness, no one is experiencing freedom; we live by making concessions, giving the reins of power to all others, instead of experiencing the search and discovery of inner expansion.

When we begin to ask ourselves, "What am I? Who am I? What is this? What are we doing here? Where did I come from and what is my destiny?" the anguish is so great that we must move in the direction of discovery. When the "I am" is discovered—and every enlightened tradition has said this—we find ourselves and we find God. Look for yourself, and you'll find your creator.

To live in a state of peace and grace means that we must let go of denial and honor all aspects of our being. We can embrace the totality of our essential expression. We can embrace third-, fourth-, and fifth-dimensional reality and keep opening to the dimensions yet beyond. We can let go of anything that says "no" to our journey. We can honor our emotional, physical, and mental bodies so they work together in harmony to express our inherent divinity.

The Now Age

Each person on the planet, and the planet itself, is in a spiritual progression, given that the distinction between live and inanimate is mere illusion. The earth pulses, feels, loves, grows, and aligns itself with the cosmos.

We are moving toward that which is sacred. It doesn't really matter whether we're returning to it or discovering it. What matters at this point in history is that we become it. And becoming it is the simplest process in life because we can only become what we are. We cannot become something else. With commitment to this journey, we can readily sort ourselves out. If we are sacred—and my postulate is that every life is sacred—then the process of discovering it, recovering it, returning to it, becoming aware of it, is the work of our lifetime. Then we can use every speck of consciousness to wake up our families, our communities, and our culture, which have been immersed in a consciousness of self-forgetting.

Indeed, authentic spirituality is not an escape from the real world. No true sage can encapsulate himself in the self-sufficiency that the New Age promotes. Spirituality is about spiritual autonomy, connection, and relationship.

We know that there are 85 billion galaxies out there, that the quartz molecule of the chromosomes represents something real, but we must have peace in ourselves, on earth, and in heaven—and not in the context of a certain level of control. Therefore a new mythology is being created. It is not a single concept of peace.

All religions are different, but all seek to eliminate the injustices, the selfishness, the greed, and the passions that stand in the way of this new mythology. When the purpose is forgotten, holy wars arise. We are a community in crisis, but this very crisis will usher us into a new era.

But before emerging into a new world order, we have to look at who we are as self-selected souls who have come to earth and who carry the miracle of life in action. All of us in this world want to feel useful, be it through service to the community, through work in our profession, or by involvement in a variety of actions. Yet first we must experience the inner reality that is a nontransferable, deep part within us—our essence, soul, Self, higher self, or whatever else we choose to call it.

No matter what system we choose to practice in order to wake up, we all must be dedicated in a transformative manner to shift the myth of our existence from a transient, limited perspective to a higher, more encompassing one. Being more knowledgeable about spiritual realities does not get the job done. We need to mutate totally and engage in actions that will enable us to be the citizens of a functional civilization (and not as what vice-president Al Gore once called this one—a dysfunctional civilization that has placed planet earth in the balance).

The human species is in the phase of adolescence in which we imagine that we should concern ourselves with other things, without worrying so much about our own self-development. But individually and collectively we find ourselves in a crucial evolutionary moment, where a leap of consciousness is critical to our survival.

To have 800 million people enduring hunger, out of 6 billion, is not an optimal existence. The transformation of consciousness implies a change of residence. We must each make ourselves a human being of the planet, at least internally, and one who is capable of perceiving with a global vision and focused action. We can participate in any zone: our job, family, office. Then we can dedicate our efforts to others in our country, region, continent, and planet.

We are one body, and it is not only a body of consciousness on the planet earth but a body of consciousness wherever there is life in the universe. If there are extraterrestrials—and who knows if there are?—and if we are all interdependent, isn't it possible that these beings could be a little annoyed about what we are doing here? Three stations from the sun, there lives a group of creatures that have a covering of grime, called smog, encircling their planet, which unbalances the oxygenation of the whole solar system. Doesn't it affect what happens on Uranus, for example?

We must begin with love. We must learn to love ourselves in spite of what we perceive as imperfections or limitations. With that love and self-acceptance, we must desire those around us to be free and empowered. Loving others as ourselves is the first step toward eliminating the human family's enslavement to matter. Without that love, we are willing all else to fail.

It is time to be working for the success of all rather than in competition with everyone. For the past 6,000 years, humans have been more interested in knocking holes in the decks of neighbors' boats than in patching up those holes. At last, as the water level is up to our eyes, we are beginning to see that we are all on the same sinking ship. We cannot save ourselves without seeking the benefit of others.

We are at the end of one age and at the beginning of another. How will the Now Age manifest itself? God only knows. The Now Age is new, and it offers us the opportunity to participate in the co-creation of the divine function, which can be manifested in plenitude.

The Now Order is free, not emotional, but clean, pure, and certain. It is light. It is not one group against another. It is cooperation, inner work, the work of love. It is the elevation of the consciousness from the material to the nuclear, from the nuclear to the atomic, from the atomic to the subatomic, to the resplendence of the electronic body of totality.

The opportunity to awaken is now. It is time to learn the basic technology that can make us human, spiritual, and multidimensional beings. The path I've described in this book is not utopia, nor is it a philosophy. It's a real process based on learning how to vibrate at higher frequencies, respectful of all dimensions of creation. When we understand how real and available this path is, we can stop marveling at how someone else is transformed and begin to align ourselves with our own possibilities for transformation.

For me, the definition of normalcy is to be an integrated human being who is in tune with the higher frequencies. My life has been directed, since I was very young, to search for the point of departure. There are few adventures in which I haven't participated in order to see how they would turn out, what kind of discomfort I would have to leave, and what I could do to avoid the same conditions another time in the evolutionary process of my soul. I have dedicated a great part of my life to investigating, to being scientific about the truth, which is the science of life. I am grateful.

My intention is that you become inspired today. I want you to mutate today. Validate that which is sacred, which is you. Activate that which is you, which is sacred. And invalidate that to which you have given false value. Let go of anything that keeps you from knowing that you are divine and deserving of a wholesome life.

The soul is fearless about change and will welcome the opportunity to dissolve whatever stands in its way. Patterns of interaction and patterns of energy that are no longer useful: farewell! The soul desires to move toward greater wholeness, letting go of self-limiting beliefs. And it supports all other beings in alignment with this purpose which is your sacred destiny.

The Keys of Being

Twelve guiding rules will help us shift into the Age of Now.

1. Always look for the good in each person, situation, or thing. It resides at the core level.
2. Resolutely turn your back on the past, be it

good or bad, and live only in the present and future.

3. Forgive all the world without exception, no matter what they've done; then forgive yourself from the fullness of your heart.

4. Consider your job, children, or daily studies as something sacred. Know that you are a magnificent contribution. Your work is a service, whatever it is, and your awareness will benefit yourself and all others.

5. Do all that is in your power to manifest a healthy body and a harmonious environment.

6. Be in the service of your being and that of your neighbor. Be an instrument for divine energy and the lessons of truth, to be taught in a discreet and knowing way.

7. Be aware of your speech. Practice silence. Unconditionally avoid criticism. Do not listen to it or support it.

8. Dedicate at least fifteen minutes of your day to meditation, inner work, spiritual exercise, and prayer.

9. Upon awakening, visualize the higher power of your choice, and offer gratitude. Upon retiring, consciously forgive yourself and others for any deviations from the path of heart.

10. Practice the Golden Rule. Do unto others as you would have them do unto you. It is important to practice this no matter how others treat you. Remember that this and all rules have their opposite, and as such, do not let others do to you what you would not do to them.

11. Know that whatever you experience can be transformed by way of prayer and meditation.

12. Ask yourself when you awake, when you fall asleep, when you leave your house, and whenever else it occurs to you, "Is my heart open?"

❖ **EXERCISE** ❖

Don't be afraid: beneath the color of your skin, your hair, your eyes, and beyond the mountain of your doubts, fears, and defenses, there is not the emptiness you fear but a presence, a truth, a happiness, well-being, and health—and above all that is what you truly are.

To get to know yourself: take a moment of silence and be internally attentive. Listen to the sound that there is in you. Meditate for a moment, through feeling your body, excluding the world of form; close your eyes and affirm deep inside:

Soul that I Am, I am not my body, nor my mind, nor my sentiments, nor my emotions; these are phenomena that I have, situations that occur in me.

Soul that I Am that which Soul that I Am, Soul that I Am, Soul that I Am, Soul that I Am, the same as I was before I was born, as a child, Soul that I Am which is here now, that which will always be, that which comes from the depths of my very heart, and sends me what I think, feel, act, and work. Soul that I Am this eternal essence that Soul that I Am always in search of.

Once you learn to live in soul consciousness and stabilize the vibration of your true name, this voice is heard clearly, and you can use the phrase "Soul that I Am" to center yourself in any activity. Thus the healing power of your sacred self will fully and consciously rule your life.

ACKNOWLEDGMENTS

———————— ❖ ————————

The threads of life weave us in ways that become evident only as we travel through the territories where they take us. Thus, now in the midst of my life when I look back at my healing and learning journey, I am filled with gratitude and reverence for the many beings who have enriched me.

At the beginning of this gratitude is the Greater Context—God—the warm and loving force-field that holds us, nourishes us, and sustains us. To the Divine I dedicate my life and work. I acknowledge this presence both day and night and give thanks for the restoration of my soul in this dimension each morning. I acknowledge the presence of the sustaining force of Mother Earth, its beauty and magnificence, from the heights of my native Andes Mountains and the vastness of the Pacific Ocean, to the rainforest of the Amazon, to the high desert of my current residence in Arizona. The heights of Machu Picchu and the Old City in Jerusalem—all these places have enriched me at different stages of my life. I give thanks to the beings of this dimension and others, forms of light experienced as visions and meditations that have opened my perception to worlds that go beyond the material dimensions of existence.

I would also like to thank my family: my late mother, who was my close friend throughout her life; my beloved father—companion, guide, and supporter—with whom I had the greatest camaraderie a son could hope for; and their parents, whose connection to a lineage has allowed me to be rooted in spirituality. I thank my beloved wife, Carolina, whose companionship and loving support is the sweetest balsam in my work and life; and our beloved children, Alexandra, Charles, and David Gabriel, whose presence touches our essence daily and inspires us to further the work for future generations.

In addition, I want to thank the teachers and friends whom I have met along the way, including His Holiness the Dalai Lama, Willis Harman, Idries Shah, Hernan Alessandri, Pablo Neruda, Rodrigo Carazo, those at the Esalen Institute, and others too numerous to mention, including my students and colleagues at Heartnet International and the World Health Foundation for Development and Peace. I also thank my assistants Fabian Di Bella, Cora Kamman, and Robert Woertz, whose loyalty and constant support I fully appreciate.

I would like to thank Brian Tart, my editor, for envisioning this book. And my fondest thoughts go to Emily Hilburn Sell, who took the manuscript and through long hours crafted a mountain of written and spoken material into its present form.

I also want to thank my wonderful friends who have healed me with their love, and the many patients, students, and clients who continually remind me of the essence of service.

Carlos Warter, M.D.

ABOUT THE AUTHOR

———————— ❧ ————————

Carlos Warter, M.D., is a trained medical doctor with Harvard postgraduate education, transpersonal psychotherapist, and the acclaimed author of *Recovery of the Sacred.* Born in Chile, he has been awarded the United Nations Peace Messenger and the Pax Mundi awards for his humanitarian efforts. He lives in Sedona, Arizona.

http://www.heart-net.com
cwartermd@aol.com
PO Box 3607
Sedona, AZ 86340